The EDINBURGH AND EAST COAST Cook Book

A celebration of the amazing food & drink on our doorstep.

The Edinburgh and East Coast Cook Book

©2019 Meze Publishing Ltd. All rights reserved.

First edition printed in 2019 in the UK.

ISBN: 978-1-910863-45-9

Thank you to: Jamie Scott, The Newport and Scott Smith, Fhior

Compiled by: Jo Mallinder

Written by: Katie Fisher

*Photography by: Clair Irwin
(www.clairirwinphotography.com)*

Edited by: Phil Turner, Chris Brierley

Designed by: Paul Cocker

*Contributors: Sarah Koriba, David Wilson,
Izzy Randall, Amy Clarke, Sam Hancock,
Sally Zaki, Vanesa Balaj, Ruth Alexander,
Amelia Brownhill*

Cover art: Luke Prest (www.lukeprest.com)

Published by Meze Publishing Limited
Unit 1b, 2 Kelham Square
Kelham Riverside
Sheffield S3 8SD
Web: www.mezepublishing.co.uk
Telephone: 0114 275 7709
Email: info@mezepublishing.co.uk

CONTENTS

FOREWORD

Despite moving about a lot when I was younger on account of my dad's army career, I knew for certain that I wanted to set up home in Scotland as a chef, even without knowing exactly where.

After I won MasterChef: The Professionals in 2014, I had a lot of different offers for work all over the UK. By this time though, I was deeply in love with the Kingdom! The Kingdom – which you should know, I hope – is the wonderful, beautiful Fife, blessed with rolling hills, stunning coastline, deep forests, white beaches and amazing farm lands. This isn't why I love the area so much…that's thanks to the sheer unrivalled passion for produce from the farmers, producers and suppliers here. It's borderline obsessive!

At the restaurant, we use as much from the region as we can. Our butcher is the great Henderson's of Glenrothes, our fish supplier is David Lowrie & Son in St Monans, we use Euan at Pittormie Farm where fruit and vegetables – from onions, squash, kale and cabbages to varieties of gooseberries, strawberries, raspberries, apples and pears – are grown all year round.

Taking time to forage is also massively important to us for pushing the food forward and as an independent business. We get beautiful sea herbs such as sea anster, samphire, salty fingers and sea purslane from the coast, and in the woodlands we're spoilt for choice with mushrooms, wild leeks, garlic and wood sorrels, to name just a few. We always try to do this as a team as it's great to get some fresh air and to bond outside as well as in the kitchen.

At The Newport, we want to showcase what Scotland has to offer produce-wise, how talented Scottish chefs are and how welcoming our front of house team are. What's great about this book is that it champions Fife producers, restaurants and suppliers and celebrates just how good this region and the east of Scotland really is.

Jamie Scott
The Newport

FOREWORD

From the age of 15, I always knew I wanted to have my own restaurant.

I feel very lucky to have achieved this, twice now. Edinburgh's not where I'm from, but it's where I've been made to feel at home. Despite being a capital city, it feels more like a small town. People know each other, and a community spirit still exists. This community could not be felt any more strongly than in the hospitality industry.

Laura and I opened our first restaurant, Norn, in 2016. Having no previous reputation in the area and setting up in a challenging location, we were completely taken back by the city's response. The restaurant very quickly gained a fantastic name for itself and we found ourselves in The Times Top 100 and the same list by Restaurant Magazine in our first year. The support we received was overwhelming, not only from our customers, but also the amazing community of other restaurants, cafés, bars and suppliers. We consider the people at many of those businesses close friends now.

Sadly, Laura and I had to make the very difficult decision to walk away from Norn and to start again, right from the beginning. We dreaded that the fallout would alienate us from much of our community as we opened our new restaurant Fhior in June 2018. We couldn't have been more wrong. The bonds and friendships we had made came out in more ways than we could have imagined, and the support was unbelievable and humbling.

I feel very privileged to have been asked to introduce this fantastic book that showcases just a portion of the amazing and growing food scene we have in Edinburgh. The produce and the passion in this city is outstanding and there are so many talented people dedicated to making Edinburgh's culinary landscape so vibrant, varied and innovative. I feel very proud to call this city my home.

Scott Smith
Fhior

Join the AKVA-PARTY

With one of Edinburgh's biggest outdoor spaces right on the waters of Union Canal, Akva is a bar and party venue with delicious food served all day, ready to welcome anyone and everyone from morning till late.

"A bar doesn't have to be just a bar" is the ethos behind the 'Boda bars' of Edinburgh, and sums Akva up pretty well. Anna and Mike are the Swedish couple and business partners behind Akva, which is one of eight venues they run in Edinburgh with the joyful aim of bringing people together. Atmosphere is very important to Anna, Mike and their teams. Though Akva, Joseph Pearce and the other Boda bars are all different in their own way, the feel of each venue is the same. Warm, inviting, cosy and homely are the buzzwords when it comes to the décor and creating a perfect melting pot of Swedish and Scottish culture to enjoy with friends old and new.

Akva's bar and restaurant extends over two levels and can host an incredible 600 guests across the downstairs and mezzanine floors. That's not even including the outdoor space – one of the city's largest beer gardens – overlooking Union Canal, in which up to 200 more people can enjoy (occasional) Scottish sunshine, Swedish lager on draft, the annual 'Canal Fest' and Swedish Midsummer parties which are a no-holds-barred celebration featuring maypoles, flower garlands, dancing, barbecues and games for kids and big kids alike.

For private events as well as regular celebrations held at Akva, there's plenty of food, filter coffee (the Swedes' typical preference) and a wide selection of drinks to wash all the fun down with. Swedish meatballs and other hearty dishes, smorrebrod (open sandwiches) and light bites, brunch and fika (a Swedish concept, meaning coffee and something sweet enjoyed on a break) make the menu an eclectic yet comforting smörgåsbord.

Providing a place for everyone to come together and have a good time bonds the staff across every venue belonging to Anna and Mike. They are genuinely invested in great hospitality, so lots of specific training is given to everyone who joins the team, and members are encouraged to help each other out while managers work closely with each other to share ideas. In 2018, two new venues joined the bunch; Sofi's Southside and Harry's definitely won't be the last Swedish-*cum*-Scottish bars to brighten Edinburgh's social scene, so watch this space for the fun to continue!

Det är
omöjligt
att
älska och
vara
förnuftig på
samma gång...

Akva
SWEDISH MEATBALLS AND CLAPSHOT POTATOES

Classic Swedish meatballs are always made with a mix of beef and pork mince and as tradition dictates, are always served with peas and jam. The spices can vary from family to family, but this is our very own Akva recipe. Rumour has it that cinnamon is an aphrodisiac so don't miss out this spice!

Preparation time: 20 minutes | Cooking time: 30 minutes | Serves: 3

Ingredients

For the meatballs:

300g pork mince

100g beef mince

½ medium-sized white onion

1 clove of garlic

8g dill, chopped

3 pinches of salt

2 pinches of ground pepper

2 pinches of ground cardamom

2 pinches of ground cinnamon

2 pinches of ground nutmeg

2 splashes of Worcestershire sauce

Drizzle of olive oil

For the clapshot potatoes:

1 medium turnip, chopped

Potatoes (same weight as turnip), chopped

Salt and pepper

Knob of butter

For the onion and dill cream sauce:

½ medium-sized white onion

1 clove of garlic

200ml white wine

Knob of butter

400ml double cream

5g dill, chopped

Salt and pepper

Method

For the meatballs

Preheat the oven to 185˚c. Mix the pork and beef mince together in a large mixing bowl. Purée the onion and garlic together in a blender, then add this to the mince. Add the dill, salt, pepper, cardamom, cinnamon, nutmeg and Worcestershire sauce to the bowl and mix everything together well. Weigh out the meatball mix into portions of 40 to 45g each, then roll into balls. Place the meatballs on a baking tray and drizzle with olive oil. Cook in the preheated oven for 14 minutes.

For the clapshot potatoes

Boil the turnip until cooked, then drain and mash. Do the same with the potatoes, combine the two and season with salt, pepper and butter to taste.

For the onion and dill cream sauce

Thinly slice the onion and crush the garlic. Lightly brown the onion and garlic together in a non-stick pan. Add the white wine and butter. Reduce the liquid by half, then add the cream and reduce again until the sauce starts to thicken. Stir through the chopped dill. Season with salt and pepper to taste.

To serve

Serve the meatballs with a side of clapshot potatoes. Cover the meatballs with a serving of onion and dill cream sauce, then garnish with a little more chopped dill.

The Perfect
PAIRING

Proudly laying claim to its status as the only haggis and whisky bar in Edinburgh, Arcade is a meeting of old and new offering fantastic food and more varieties of scotch than you can shake a tumbler at.

Arcade Bar, Haggis and Whisky House has seen more than 12 years of guests tread the cobbles of Cockburn Street to pay this Edinburgh institution a visit. Anna Brudnowska and her partner Ewa opened the venture in 2006 and have transformed a very old, run-down pub into a thriving hub for haggis and whisky lovers. It stemmed from the pairing of two Scottish favourites and has become incredibly popular, even becoming the top spot in the city, by recommendation, to enjoy a plateful of haggis.

The building that now houses Arcade was home to one of Edinburgh's oldest pubs and is listed to protect some beautiful original features, which Anna and Ewa celebrated and showcased in their renovation. The name and the old stone walls remain recognisable, but the experienced pair have added their own flair and contemporary touches to the interiors and food and drink menus.

"We try to make everything on the premises," says Anna, "even down to the sauces, which are never bought in." It's good hearty pub food with a few twists, arriving in big portions and featuring some of Scotland's best produce. "We look for the best butchers and fishmongers, never use big chains, enjoy sourcing locally – mostly within the city – and find organic options when we can," explains Anna. The aim is to continually improve the taste and quality of the food, so despite its longevity, Arcade never stands still in its mission to create a unique experience for anyone to enjoy.

Whisky is the bar's main focus, of course, with over 100 options that include Speyside, Islay and Highland malts as well as speciality whiskies such as the vintage Secret Stills bottling, distilled at an anonymous Scottish distillery in 1966. There's also a select range of beers, including one brewed especially for Arcade named Haggis Hunter.

The welcoming atmosphere reflects the pub's approach to food; contemporary presentation of tradition is evident in the décor and homely yet smart-looking dishes. "The contrast in our looks and menu has something to please all tastes," says Anna. "We like to showcase the old and the new, keeping history alive while always improving and looking forward."

Arcade Bar
PRINCESS DIANA HAGGIS WITH DRAMBUIE WHISKY LIQUEUR

There are two types of people in this world: the ones who love haggis and the ones who hate it! We love haggis so much that we've decided to make it our prime ingredient and the most important dish in the restaurant...and (in not only our opinion) we pulled it off beautifully! Enjoy recreating this delicious dish at home.

Preparation time: 15 minutes | Cooking time: 40 minutes | Serves: 2

Ingredients

1 tbsp olive oil

½ onion, finely chopped

100g button mushrooms, finely chopped

1 tomato, finely chopped

30ml Drambuie whisky

125ml pouring cream

Sea salt and freshly ground black pepper, to taste

350g hot mashed potato

350g hot mashed turnip

350g hot cooked peeled and crumbled haggis

Parsley, to garnish

Method

Heat the oil in a frying pan over a medium heat. Add the onion and stir for 2 minutes or until soft. Add the mushrooms and cook for another minute, then add the tomato and cook for another 2 minutes or until soft. Add the whisky, then gently tilt the pan toward the flame until the alcohol ignites. When the flames have subsided, stir in the cream. Reduce the heat to low, season to taste and simmer for 1 minute or until slightly thickened. Remove from the heat and keep warm.

Place an 8cm deep by 10cm wide round stainless steel ring onto a serving plate. Spoon half of the mashed potato into the mould and press it down tightly, then repeat with half the mashed turnip, then half the haggis. You should have three nice even layers. Remove the mould from the plate, then repeat on a second plate with the remaining mash and haggis. Divide the sauce between the plates, scatter with parsley and serve immediately.

A tea-time
TRADITION

Charm, china and good old-fashioned home cooking await you in abundance at Clarinda's Tea Room, still going strong after more than 40 years on Edinburgh's Royal Mile.

Clarinda's Tea Room takes a refreshingly quaint approach to café culture in the heart of Edinburgh's Old Town. Homely and hearty food and drink is served amid 'olde-worldy' décor and plenty of friendly conversation between guests sharing tables in the cosy interior. As it only seats 30 people at a time, yet has a reputation built on decades of returning customers, Clarinda's has queues out the door during Edinburgh's busiest months. Out of the tourist season though, there's ample opportunity to enjoy the tea room's quieter moments too, with classical music in the background and space to while away a relaxing afternoon with a cup of tea and a book.

As one of the oldest businesses on the Royal Mile, Clarinda's has plenty of its own history but is also grounded in the area's literary heritage. Clarinda (whose real name was Agnes Maclehose) was a close friend of Scotland's national poet, Robert Burns, and inspired his popular love song Ae Fond Kiss. The pair exchanged a number of romantic letters under pseudonyms; Clarinda for her and Sylvander for him. She is buried in the neighbouring Canongate Church Kirkyard, commemorated by a memorial plaque.

The tea room was established in 1976 by Marion Thomson and has remained largely unchanged, keeping all the little touches that gave Clarinda's its charm and appeal from the beginning. Today's owner, Maggie Dowdell, is a former employee who has run the business since 2013. The focus is still on a range of delicious cakes and scones baked in the tea room and displayed temptingly on a cake stand, accompanied by loose leaf tea served with all the proper paraphernalia: teapots, strainers, delicate cups and saucers.

The menus are made up of "things people recognise, that you'd expect to find in your gran's recipe book," says Maggie. The small team do all the baking in-house with eggs from a farm in East Lothian, and enjoy creating a friendly atmosphere to complement their comforting homemade breakfasts, lunches and sweet treats which people return for again and again.

Clarinda's Tea Room
GINGERBREAD

This recipe produces a dark, sticky loaf that is kept moist by the abundance of treacle. Delicious alone or served warm with a generous spread of butter.

Preparation time: 10 minutes | Cooking time: approximately 45 minutes | Serves: 8

Ingredients

230g plain flour

120g soft margarine

60g sugar

175g treacle

60g golden syrup

2 large eggs

5g bicarbonate of soda

5g mixed spice

15g ground ginger

125ml whole milk

Method

Preheat the oven to 180°c (fan) then grease and flour a 2lb loaf tin, or use a loaf tin liner.

Place the flour, margarine, sugar, treacle, golden syrup, eggs, bicarbonate of soda and spices into the bowl of an electric mixer. Beat on a medium speed for 5 minutes until the mixture is smooth and glossy.

Slowly add the milk while mixing continuously. Pour the mixture into the prepared loaf tin and bake for approximately 45 minutes.

Cool the loaf on a wire rack before cutting into thick slices and enjoying!

Variations

For an even deeper flavour, add a few pieces of finely chopped stem ginger to the mixture before baking. Alternatively, try adding a small handful of crystallised ginger pieces to the mixture before baking for a chewy, sweet addition. The loaf is even more delicious with a layer of glacé icing on top.

Catch of THE DAY

Based in St Monans – one of the East Neuk of Fife's historic fishing villages – David Lowrie Fish Merchants provides the very best wild Scottish seafood for establishments on the east coast and across central Scotland.

The Lowrie family are now in their fourth generation of fish merchants, and their current business was founded over 30 years ago by David Lowrie. The family-run business is still thriving thanks to David, his son Lewis and brother Edward working together to source and deliver fresh fish and seafood to many restaurants, hotels and chip shops across Scotland. The aim of the fish merchants is to make sure the produce they provide is of the best quality and has the least amount of time between catch and kitchen. This is only possible because of the fishermen and buyers on the markets, most of whom have had a working relationship with the merchants for over 30 years and are able to source fish directly off the boats in many cases, across the coasts of Scotland and as far up as the Shetlands.

The merchants then take the best catches of the day from the buyers and process orders themselves. Only the top quality fish are chosen from the catch, as each one is quality checked by a member of the Lowrie family and individually handpicked before being packaged for their clients. The team personally keep in contact with every client they sell to, working closely with chefs to provide them with the best seafood that the Scottish coast has to offer. The Lowries have a strong belief in working with the changing seasons and always using the most sustainable produce available. This whole process, with the fish merchants acting as an efficient middle man between the fisherman and the chef, means that fish are usually landed, on the market and in the kitchen within 24 hours.

Underlying this whole process is the passion that David and his family have for effectively sourcing and providing the freshest wild seafood and shellfish. This in turn showcases how fantastic Scotland's produce really is. Having grown up in a fishing village himself, David understands the importance his business has in promoting the many thriving fishing villages across the country that are able to provide fish for Scottish businesses. By maintaining this successful business model, the Lowries try their best to set the standard for how fish should be sourced: locally and seasonally.

David Lowrie Fish Merchants

David Lowrie
Fish Merchants
SPAGHETTI VONGOLE

This recipe comes from years ago, and would be enjoyed on our last supply stop when returning from Edinburgh after a busy morning and lunch service. Myself, the chef Danny and his longest regular customer John would sit and share a hearty bowl of pasta. I'd supply the clams and Danny would cook up this wonderful dish. It has stuck with me ever since and I continue to cook it to this day.

Preparation time: 10 minutes, plus 1 hour for cleaning clams | Cooking time: 10 minutes | Serves: 4

Ingredients

2kg clams (we recommend surf or palourde clams)

½ lemon, juiced

500g spaghetti

1 tbsp olive oil

2 cloves of garlic

½ tsp dried or fresh red chilli

125ml dry white wine

1 bunch of fresh parsley

Method

Submerge the clams in cold water with the juice of half a lemon to clean them, and leave to soak for 1 hour. Change the water twice during this time.

Bring a large pot of salted water up to the boil. Add the spaghetti and cook until al dente.

In the meantime, heat the olive oil in a large frying pan on a low heat then add the garlic and chilli, making sure not to colour the garlic. Add the drained clams and the wine, cover the pan and bring to the boil. Steam for 2 to 3 minutes or until all the clams have opened. Stir through the parsley and finally add the cooked pasta to the pan. Stir for 1 minute to combine. Check the seasoning and add a little more olive oil if needed. Serve straightaway and enjoy!

Chef's tip: adding lemon to the water for cleaning clams is important because the acidity helps to remove all remaining grit from the clams.

A sweeter kind of MIXOLOGY

Eat Me by Lesley specialises in customised cakes that taste like your favourite cocktail, all designed, baked and delivered by the venture's enterprising founder...

What could be more fun than cake and cocktails? Cocktail-flavoured cakes, of course! Eat Me by Lesley is a one-woman show providing a made-to-order cake service for any occasion that calls for such a deliciously decadent combo. Lesley set up the venture in 2015, following her heart in a complete change of career, knowing only that she wanted to give people a unique experience by helping customers find the perfect cake so they can provide a great memory on special occasions. Lesley taught herself to bake and began taking orders through the business' Facebook page, which quickly grew as she became known for quality cake creations.

"I didn't want it to turn into a conveyor belt of cakes though," she explains, as keeping Eat Me small also meant keeping it special, thanks to cakes that are always freshly made, personalised to each customer, and even delivered by Lesley herself. She often travels across the country, carefully transporting cakes to weddings, hen parties, girl's nights and other celebrations in Edinburgh and sometimes far beyond.

Her designs stem from the first step in the cake-creating process: a brief from the customer on the style and flavour they're after as well as how many people it needs to serve and how long Lesley has to create it. This can include gluten-free cakes as well as plain or alternative options. She does have a menu of half a dozen flavours based on classic cocktails and re-named with inspiration from Alice in Wonderland, but enjoys the fun of "making people's dreams come true" by putting her own twist on existing designs and tailoring each creation to the individual.

This attention to detail extends right to the ingredients; she has organic eggs delivered from a farm just outside Edinburgh and always looks for the highest quality products – such as Scottish butter – to incorporate. Lesley has worked on collaborations with various alcohol brands and has more in the pipeline for 2019, which will also see her first sales through a newly formed cake ordering platform backed by Just Eat, as well as sales through another great cake ordering platform, Mums Bake Cakes. Her cakes also recently became available in Leaf & Bean Café on Comiston Road. From the beginnings of an idea to a thriving country-wide venture, Eat Me by Lesley is the go-to for those who, like the woman behind it all, just love cocktails and cake!

Eat Me by Lesley

HATTER'S TEA PARTY

Everyone loves a Long Island Iced Tea and now you can make one in your own home. I love this recipe because it combines some of the best spirits for you to ice onto a perfectly baked cake.

Preparation time: 10-15 minutes | Cooking time: 20-25 minutes | Serves: 12

Ingredients

For the cakes:

250g caster sugar

250g Stork, at room temperature

250g self-raising flour

4 large eggs, at room temperature

For the icing:

250g unsalted butter

600g icing sugar

20ml vodka

20ml rum

20ml Cointreau

60ml cola

Method

Preheat the oven to 150°c.

For the cakes

Beat the sugar and Stork together until smooth, then add the flour and all the eggs and mix again until smooth. Divide the mixture between 12 large cupcake cases. Bake in the preheated oven for approximately 20 to 25 minutes and take out when golden and spongy to the touch.

For the icing

Beat the butter until smooth, then add 500g of icing sugar and beat again to combine until smooth. Add the spirits and mix until thoroughly blended together. You may need to add the remaining 100g of icing sugar at this stage to ensure that the icing isn't too watery.

Once mixed together and of fairly thick consistency, put the icing into a piping bag with a nozzle. Pipe onto the cooled cupcakes then sit back and enjoy your creation!

Hearth & HOME

Scottish produce, social enterprise, and a passion for cooking great food permeate every aspect of the award-winning café and takeaway, Edinburgh Larder.

Edinburgh Larder was created to be – as its name suggests – a hub for people who live and work in the city as well as tourists, giving everyone a flavour of what Scottish food is really about. Owner Eleanor Cunningham felt there wasn't enough representation for her home country's fantastic produce around the Royal Mile despite it being well-known and much-visited. So, after gaining varied experience in business and deciding that starting her own venture was the next step, Eleanor opened the café and takeaway in 2009.

From the very beginning, working closely with suppliers was a key part of Edinburgh Larder's ethos. "We enjoy collaborating with the smaller scale growers and producers to plan our menus, featuring seasonal produce in flexible dishes like platters of local charcuterie or cheese, soups, salads and tarts that reflect what's available naturally in the countryside around us," says Eleanor. Visits to these suppliers, and tasting sessions for the team, are an important step on their path to delicious fresh food and drink. In 2018 they even started roasting their own coffee, and have long been famed across Edinburgh for a cracking brunch featuring homemade baked beans and organic sausage rolls that are made – amongst many hearty dishes, jams and chutneys, cakes and other sweet treats – entirely in-house. They also make their own gluten-free bread and feature a wide range of vegetarian and vegan dishes as well as dishes for meat lovers.

The emphasis on making good food from scratch stems from Eleanor's childhood, since her family have always been real foodies and she was inspired to begin cooking at home with the bounty of her parents' big vegetable garden. She's now committed to extending that same inspiration to others through a social enterprise that encompasses classes and workshops across Edinburgh, delivered via a food truck from primary schools to community gardens. "It brought out the best in our chefs and the people they were teaching," says Eleanor, "as the whole idea is to make cooking fun, accessible and affordable by working with seasonal produce and so reducing that distance between what we're eating and the ingredients themselves."

The cheerful, bright and airy space at Edinburgh Larder has a creative feel to it that reflects the team's attitude to food and its origins. Catering for events and corporate lunches takes this even further into the city, providing everything a larder should for people across Edinburgh: a vital part of any home, reflecting the landscape and providing the raw materials and ideas for great cooking.

Edinburgh Larder
RHUBARB CORDIAL

We love rhubarb cordial at the larder because it uses one of the best and most versatile seasonal fruits, and reminds us a bit of rhubarb and custard sweets! This is a lovely recipe to make with kids and much tastier than cordials you can buy in the shops. It's a great way of preserving rhubarb (or any seasonal fruit) so you can make as much as you like and enjoy it all year round.

Preparation time: approximately 15 minutes, plus overnight straining | Cooking time: 1 hour
Makes about 1 litre of cordial (at least 30 drinks, depending on how strong you like them to be!)

Ingredients

3kg rhubarb

1.8 litres water

Caster sugar, as required (see method)

3 lemons

Method

Roughly chop the rhubarb and place in a large pan with the water. Bring the mixture to a gentle boil and then simmer for approximately 45 minutes.

Use a potato masher to crush and break down the fruit until totally soft. Place a large sieve over a clean pan and line it with muslin or similar fine cloth. Strain the mixture through the muslin overnight.

Measure the volume of liquid collected and add 700g of caster sugar for every litre of liquid. Warm the mixture gently in a pan to dissolve the sugar and add freshly squeezed lemon juice to taste.

Bottle while warm in sterilised bottles.

Once the bottles are open, store in the fridge and use within three months. Enjoy the cordial with still or sparkling water or in a cocktail of your choice; it's great with fizz!

A CUT ABOVE

The Brazilian rodizio extended its authentic gaúcho experience to Edinburgh in February 2018, bringing together Scottish heritage and South American tradition.

Fazenda draws on the lifestyle and cuisine of South America's gaúchos to create an experience centred around food and sharing at each of its five restaurants across the UK. The Edinburgh venue is one of the more recently opened, and links in with the ethos and core values of the business while adding a few unique touches of its own.

The name is Portuguese in origin, meaning a large estate or farm which is where all the traditions start from. Gaúchos – Argentinian and southern Brazilian 'cowboys' – would cook their meat skewered on long wooden stakes stuck into the ground surrounding an open fire, roasting it slowly out of direct heat so the cuts stayed juicy and tender until they were ready to break from their work and eat together. This practice would be replicated at weekends with family, drinking wine or maté while preparing the delicious hearty meals.

It's this experience that Fazenda brings to guests in Edinburgh, with a little more modern sophistication. Whole pieces of meat are cooked on skewers then brought out and carved at the table as they are ready. Up to 15 mouth-watering options, from beef skirt and chicken hearts to the signature cut Picanha (cap of rump), are offered alongside a generous table of hot and cold gourmet sides. Feijoada is one of these; a traditional Brazilian rich black bean and meat stew with humble origins that packs in huge depth of flavour. Freshly chopped salads, breads, cured meats and continental cheeses plus vegan, vegetarian and pescetarian dishes bring the number of choices to over 50 for sharing and trying with friends and loved ones.

"Fazenda exists to make guests feel special," says Natalia, the brand manager and one of a core team passionate about making the restaurants a true representation of the way they approach food. Executive chef Fran was especially keen to work with local farmers around Edinburgh, so the branch has a 'Butcher's Choice' cut on the menu that always comes from Scottish produce. "Every member of staff knows who we are and why we do what we do," explains Natalia. "When we find people as invested as we are, to create new memories and moments of sharing and experience for our guests, that is gold to us."

Fazenda
PICANHA ASSADA

This recipe is part of a tasting menu curated by Francisco Martinez, Fazenda's executive chef, which displays a modern approach to classic recipes from Brazil. It also showcases the chef's expertise, who has a Michelin star background and has worked in kitchens around the world, including at El Bulli in Spain. That expertise is now used to source the best meats internationally and create seasonal salads for Fazenda restaurants.

Preparation time: 15 minutes, plus at least 4 hours marinating | Cooking time: 3 hour | Serves: 2

Ingredients

For the steak:

10g smoked paprika

2g salt

225g picanha steak (cap of rump)

For the roast pepper emulsion:

200g red pepper

10g garlic, peeled

20g pickled onion

10g olive oil

20g vinegar (from the pickled onions)

2g salt

For the sous vide egg:

10g salt

1 free-range egg

For the charcoal breadcrumbs:

100g strong flour

2g bamboo charcoal powder

5g salt

5g olive oil

50g water

For the rice cracker:

50g Arborio rice

200g water

10g salt

Method

For the steak

Mix the paprika and salt and then rub into both sides of the steak. Cover with cling film and leave in the fridge for a minimum of 3 hours. Take out from the fridge 1 hour before cooking to bring it down to room temperature.

Cook on a very hot skillet for 2 minutes on each side for a medium rare steak. The paprika rub will start to catch, creating a barbecue flavour. Leave to rest for the same amount of time as it was cooked before slicing to serve.

For the roast pepper emulsion

First, chargrill the red peppers. The best way of doing this is over an open fire, but if that's not an option, charring them very close to the grill in the oven will also work. Leave to cool down and once at room temperature, place them in a food processor with the other ingredients and blend for about 2 minutes. Pour through a sieve to achieve a smooth texture and keep refrigerated until serving.

For the sous vide egg

Preheat the water bath to 64°c then add the salt to the water and submerge the egg for exactly 45 minutes. This timing and temperature will give you an egg with a set white and runny yolk. This can be done in advance and reheated, but never over 60°c.

For the charcoal breadcrumbs

Combine the wet and dry ingredients in separate bowls, then stir everything together. Spread the mixture out on a flat tray and cook in the oven at 160°c for 20 minutes. Leave to cool down then place in a food processor for just 20 seconds to make the breadcrumbs.

For the rice cracker

Place the rice and water in a pot and cook for 40 minutes at a simmer. Pour the cooked rice with any remaining water into the food processor and blend to a paste. Spread this over a silicone baking mat and dehydrate at 50°c for 3 hours. Break into irregular shards and place into an airtight container. Fry the crackers as you need them in sunflower oil at 190°c for about 10 seconds.

To assemble

I like to first create a splash on the plate with the cold roast pepper emulsion, then carefully break the egg, place it on the plate and cover it with the breadcrumbs. Slice the steak as you like and top with rice crackers to bring texture to the dish.

A true taste of
SCOTLAND

Fine food and hospitality delivered with passion and skill, but without pretension: this is Fhior's trademark and underpins the ethos that permeates the modern Scottish restaurant.

Partners Scott and Laura set up Fhior in June 2018 to move in a direction that was true to their beliefs and standards when it comes to hospitality and good food. They left their previous restaurant, Norn, which won Scottish Restaurant of the Year the day before their departure! Fhior is a reflection of their desire to represent a very personal ethos both on the plate and through the service; the restaurant's name is adapted from a Gaelic word meaning true which sums up their style rather nicely.

"We're all about serious food and serious wine, but we really don't want to take ourselves too seriously," says Scott, the chef behind Fhior's three menus. Dinner is four or seven set courses, which places the diner's trust in the chefs who explain each course as it arrives without revealing what's cooking in advance. The dishes are constantly evolving and are developed around the best produce available at the time. Scott describes his food as hyper seasonal and his cooking as very reactive, using produce delivered from small local suppliers, as well as emphasising that its roots are firmly in Scotland, though you might spot the odd Nordic influence too.

Clean, clear, and pared back are words that apply to the flavours, the atmosphere and the décor at Fhior. The relatively small space can accommodate about 30 guests who are looked after from start to finish by a team of 12. There's a bar area serving drinks and snacks (of the very best kind; don't go expecting spicy nuts and pork scratchings) which they plan to develop in the future, keeping in mind the little details that transform a great experience into an outstanding one. "We try to pay attention to our customers without intruding, bringing back what we think of as 'proper' hospitality."

This approach enables Fhior to tailor its dining experience to each guest, relying on informal yet knowledgeable and skilled staff as much as the vibrant cuisine. Despite only being open a matter of months, the restaurant has already been recommended by the 2019 Michelin Guide and has promised Edinburgh a strong identity alongside an honest – you might best say truthful – offering of quality Scottish food.

Fhior

VENISON, SMOKED BEETROOT, FERMENTED SPROUTS & LIQUORICE

This dish stems from a desire to take some well-known and expected winter ingredients and elevate them to a point that brings out unrecognisable characters. The way the beetroot is cooked gives it a meaty texture and savoury smokiness, and the sprouts are fermented to create little sauerkrauts. The overall result creates a dish that looks recognisable when presented, but surprises you when you taste it. The unusual addition of liquorice creates a cooling sensation in the mouth which lightens what could be a heavy plate of food.

Preparation time: 4-6 days | Cooking time: 1 hour 30 minutes | Serves: 6

Ingredients

For the fermented sprouts:

400g sprouts

8g sea salt

For the beetroot:

2 large red beetroots

250g beef fat

2 large golden beetroot

30g oak chips

For the carrot purée:

1 large carrot

200g butter

5g powdered liquorice root

For the venison:

6 x 120g venison loins

Salt, to season

700ml venison stock

To serve:

Scurvy grass, to garnish (optional)

Method

For the fermented sprouts

Cut the sprouts in half and remove outer layers. Massage in the sea salt and leave at room temperature for 1 hour. Then pack them into jars and top up with water to just cover. Use a weight to keep them submerged and leave for 4-6 days until sour.

For the beetroots

Peel the red beetroots and slice into 1cm thick rounds. Cut them in half and trim so they're all same size. Juice the trimmings and keep the juice aside. Put the halved slices in a pan and cook in the beef fat gently for 1 hour until well cooked. Then remove from the fat and put into a low oven for about 2 hours to dry them out. Now gently heat them in the beetroot juice to soften them again. Season and keep warm.

Cook the golden beetroot covered in water for about 1 hour until just tender. Remove from the water and rub off the skin. Place in the smoker with the oak chips and smoke for 5 minutes until quite heavy on the smoke. Slice very thinly and cut into thin strips like spaghetti. Season and keep warm.

For the carrot purée

Peel and thinly slice the carrot then cook down with 150g of the butter and the liquorice. Continue to cook until completely soft and collapsed. Put into a blender and purée until smooth, adding a little water if needed. Season and keep warm.

For the venison

Heat a thick-based saucepan on a very high heat and add a little oil. When it's smoking, add the venison and sear on all sides until well-coloured. Season, turn the heat down and then add the remaining butter. Baste the meat and cook for about 6 to 8 minutes. Remove from the pan and rest. Drain the oil from the pan and deglaze with the stock. Reduce until thickened to create a sauce.

To serve

Place a spoonful of the purée on the plate with a slice of red beetroot and a nest of the golden beetroot next to it. Warm the fermented sprouts in a little butter and divide between the plates. Slice the venison and place on top of the beetroot nest. Finish with the sauce and some scurvy grass if using.

Time
FOR TEE

Housed in a unique 19th century factory, Forgan's brings the best of Scottish culture to St Andrews with quality food, live music events and a friendly welcome.

Opened in 2013, Forgan's St Andrews was established by a Glasgow-based company who specialise in turning venues with plenty of character and potential into restaurants, bars and similar ventures. In its former life, the St Andrews eatery was a golf club (or cleek) factory owned by the Forgan family, hence its name which preserves the listed building's unusual history. The restaurant showcases a large and airy dining space with industrial design features, big windows and high ceilings hung with lanterns. Smaller dining rooms, fondly referred to as bothies, have been created around the central area and are perfect for small groups to enjoy a more private dining experience.

Forgan's offers food not only throughout the day but throughout the entire year, all 365 days of it! Brunch, lunch and dinner menus reflect the restaurant's ethos, which is to preserve and celebrate Scottish heritage by serving customers traditional food such as cullen skink, neeps and tatties and of course haggis – sourced from the Isle of Arran and approved in person by the head chef – alongside familiar British and European classics: quality dishes without the fuss. Sourcing fresh and local produce is important; the fruit and veg are even proudly displayed to visitors in the passage which draws you to the entrance of the restaurant. The bar is also well stocked with home-grown products such as Scottish craft beers, lots of gin and a wee dram or two of whisky.

What goes better with good food and drink than a rousing evening of foot-stomping music? Every Thursday evening Forgan's supports local bands and artists by hosting an acoustic night, and every Friday and Saturday the famous Forgan's ceilidh draws tourists and regulars alike for an experience not to be missed. Such a fantastic atmosphere wouldn't exist without the close-knit team at Forgan's. Family-friendly service and a warm welcome for everyone is their focus, and the proof of their hard work is evident on buzzing Hogmanay nights, cheery Christmas days and throughout the bustling summer months. Forgan's is always a hit with tourists, and returning faces become regulars as the food speaks for itself and the lively calendar of events makes this restaurant the place to be in St Andrews.

Forgan's
DUCK SHEPHERD'S PIE

Why not impress the family and try something different with our homely melt in the mouth duck shepherd's pie recipe. This pie is one of our signature dishes at Forgan's and is prepared and presented in a clean and simple way where the ingredients speak for themselves!

Preparation time: 30 minutes | Cooking time: 3 hours 30 minutes | Serves: 5

Ingredients

For the confit duck:

5 duck legs

4 cloves of garlic, sliced into strips

Salt and pepper

For the jus:

250ml red wine

250ml water

200g onions, chopped

8g cornflour, mixed with a little water

For the mashed potato:

1½kg potatoes

100g unsalted butter

150ml double cream

For the lentils and bacon:

500g Puy lentils, cooked

250g smoky bacon

Method

For the confit duck

Place the duck legs on an ovenproof tray and season with the garlic, salt and pepper. Cover with the oil and place in a preheated oven at 150°c for 3 hours. Remove from the oven to cool and drain the oil. When cooled, shred the meat off the duck legs (this should be easy and the meat should just fall off the bones). Set aside.

For the jus

Place the red wine, water and onions into a pan, and simmer on the hob until reduced by half. Thicken with the cornflour paste then strain the mixture, retaining all the liquid. You should be left with 250ml of jus for the pie mixture.

For the mashed potato

Wash, peel and chop the potatoes into evenly sized chunks, place in a large pan and cover with cold water. Bring to the boil and cook for 20 minutes. Drain off the water and mash the potatoes. Stir in the butter and cream. Season with salt and pepper and set aside.

For the lentils and bacon

Cook the lentils according to the packet; we soak them first then place them in a large pot and simmer until soft. Fry the bacon and set aside.

To assemble

Mix the shredded duck meat, cooked lentils and jus. Put into a pie dish and place the sliced bacon strips on top. Cover with the mashed potato. Chef's tip: add some cheese on top of the mashed potato. Place the pie in a preheated oven at 190°c for approximately 30 minutes until the centre reaches 82°c and the cheese, if you have added some, is golden. We like to serve the pie with buttered green vegetables and thyme-infused gravy.

Flying ahead of THE FLOCK

Gannet and Guga, a gourmet sandwich bar under one of Edinburgh's East Market Street Arches, is run by a passionate team putting the creativity back into lunch on the wing.

When Malcolm Elder and Peter Millar found a location in Edinburgh's beautiful 19th century brickwork arches, their small business idea began to take shape. Lunch in the city was about to be revitalised, in the form of gourmet sandwiches plus a range of hot and cold options not limited to Vietnamese street food, rich stews, hearty soups and locally sourced cakes and sweets. Gannet and Guga opened in April 2016 under its small but perfectly formed curving roof, which the team hand-decorated with over 500 paper birds. Influences from Malcolm's travels, combined with his years of experience in hospitality, made the lunch stop stand out from the start, as did the commitment to top-notch service.

Though the venue – essentially an open kitchen with seating for a handful of customers – is mainly for takeaway food and drink, the team pride themselves on creating a really friendly and welcoming atmosphere. "We think great service is so important," says Malcolm, "and our regulars seem to appreciate it; people are always stopping by for a blether!" From cooking to conversation, everyone does everything at Gannet and Guga – everyone being Jennifer, Simona, Beth and Phil as well as the two founders – with an emphasis on doing it all really well, from scratch.

Having settled on pressure cookers to get maximum flavour out of great ingredients (and use their limited space efficiently) the sandwich aficionados make classics with inventive twists, the components for build-your-own banh mi full of punchy Asian flavours, Vietnamese summer rolls, daily salads and pulled meats, all given extra zip and zing with sauces, condiments and pickles made in-house. Bread is delivered fresh every morning from a nearby bakery – the best and most local they could find, which goes for the majority of suppliers they work with – and single origin coffee roasted in Scotland is served filter style.

Between Malcolm's fascination with Vietnamese cuisine and Peter's love of warming soups and stews, flavours are "never too crazy or inaccessible" to be added into the mix in Gannet and Guga's kitchen. They try hard to cater for everyone, dietary requirements included, and are keen to expand their thriving business in the near future, bringing the same ethos on a larger scale to more of Edinburgh's lucky lunchtime punters.

Gannet and Guga
GINGER TOFU BANH MI

After spending two months in Vietnam eating an array of the most wonderful food in the world, we decided to try making our own banh mi in Edinburgh. This classic breakfast sandwich is so versatile and includes all the flavours of Asia in an easy-to-transport form. If you don't like the idea of tofu, you can use grilled chicken, cooked haggis, pâté or deep fried fish. Anything goes! Try with kimchi or a pickle of your choice too. It really is the gift that keeps on giving!

Preparation time: 2 hours minimum | Cooking time: 10 minutes (if cooking tofu) | Serves: 4-6

Ingredients

½ large or 1 small daikon radish

2 large carrots

1 tsp table salt

150ml distilled white vinegar

200ml water

4 tbsp sugar

4cm piece of ginger root, grated and squeezed (retain the liquid)

2 tbsp soy sauce

1 tbsp maple syrup

1 tbsp sesame oil

1 pack firm tofu, drained and then pressed for 1 hour

Pinch of black pepper

To serve:

2 crusty baguettes, cut into individual portions

Maggi seasoning

Garlic mayonnaise (can be homemade or store bought)

Sriracha chilli sauce or bird's eye chillies, sliced (as much as you dare)

Small bunch of coriander, mint, thai basil or all three

Vegetarian haggis or mushroom pâté (optional)

Method

Cut the daikon radish and carrots into 3 to 5cm long and half cm thick matchsticks. Mix well with the salt and leave for 30 minutes, stirring once halfway through. Drain and lightly rinse the radish and carrot then pack them into a large jar. Mix the vinegar, water and sugar together and stir to dissolve the sugar. Pour this brine over the vegetables, pressing down as needed to fully submerge them. The resulting pickles can be eaten within the hour but are best if left until the next day. They should last up to 4 weeks in the fridge.

Mix the ginger juice, soy sauce, maple syrup and sesame oil well. Slice the pressed tofu 1cm thick, then lay the slices in a shallow dish. Cover with the ginger marinade and leave for 1 hour for the tofu to absorb it. This can be eaten raw or fried until golden brown if preferred (we think hot is best).

To serve

Cut the baguettes lengthways and shake a small dash of the Maggi seasoning onto the bread. Spread one side with a thick layer of the garlic mayo, add the tofu, top with pickles and then serve the sandwiches with the other condiments on the table for people to pick and choose. Enjoy one of the best sandwiches of your life!

Chef's tip:

Use only small amounts of the pâté or haggis if including as they are strong flavours that can take over. Vietnamese food tends to be fresh and flavourful with lots of herbs so be bold with these!

Food makes MISO HAPPY

Harajuku Kitchen started life as a Japanese street food stall in Edinburgh, and is now a renowned restaurant, being recognised as one of the 20 best restaurants in Edinburgh by Condé Nast.

Japanese entrepreneur and chef Kaori Simpson was born in Hong Kong into an expat Japanese family of merchants; her father was an international tuna trader and her Samurai great-grandfather started his own traditional fine dining Japanese restaurant. Kaori grew up helping in her mum's restaurants, learning the family recipes and eventually cooking in the kitchen, so it was almost inevitable that she would one day bring those Japanese flavours back into her life.

That journey began with gyoza dumplings and udon noodle stir fries, made and sold on a stall at the prestigious Stockbridge Market. They quickly became incredibly popular, and Edinburgh's first authentic Japanese restaurant, Harajuku Kitchen, opened in 2013. The menu features a wide range of classic Japanese dishes including sushi, katsu curries, noodle dishes and regional specialities inspired by executive chef Kaori's annual trips to Japan as well as the family recipes that have been passed down the generations to her.

The authenticity of Harajuku's cuisine has been recognised by many groups and organisations, such as the Consulate General of Japan for which the restaurant is official caterer, the Scottish Japan Society, the Japanese Chamber of Commerce in Scotland, and most recently the national Scottish Rugby Union. It shows that truly authentic Japanese cooking is in demand in Scotland, not just 'fusion confusion' Asian food.

"If you think of the best Scottish comfort food like cullen skink and mince and tatties, then that is what you will find in Harajuku Kitchen, only the food is Japanese," says Kaori. "I think no matter what country you are from, everyone understands good, homemade food that is made with love, even if you have never tried it before."

The business has many other accolades to its name, including an AA Rosette and the title of Best Japanese Restaurant at the Asian Curry Awards. It also won a Flavours of the World award from The Scottish Food and Drinks Awards, and Best Street Food in Scotland at 2018 The Scotsman Food and Drink Awards. Harajuku Kitchen is now an integral member of Edinburgh's foody and local community, serving food that makes everyone feel wholesome and happy when they taste a bite of Japan in Scotland.

Harajuku Kitchen
OYAKODON

Japanese lunch isn't just about ramen and onigiri; the menu extends to bento boxes and donburi (rice bowl) meals too. During lunch time in Japan, you will see office workers, families and housewives getting together all around town for their weekday meet ups. Our favourite lunch time meal, and one of the most popular dishes at our Edinburgh Bistro, is this oyakodon (meaning 'parent and child' because chicken and egg are used in the recipe).

Preparation time: 10 minutes | Cooking time: 12 minutes | Serves: 2

Ingredients

150ml dashi stock (1 tbsp kombu dashi or katsuo stock, dissolved in hot water)

1 tbsp light soy sauce

1 tbsp mirin (sweet rice wine)

Pinch of sugar

200g chicken thigh, cut into 3–5cm strips

1 white onion, thinly sliced

2 eggs, lightly beaten

500g cooked Japanese rice

1 spring onion or a small bunch of watercress

Pinch of nori flakes (dried seaweed)

Pinch of shichimi (Japanese blend of seven spices)

Method

Combine the dashi stock with the soy sauce, mirin, and sugar in a small saucepan. Simmer until all the sugar dissolves.

Stir in the chicken and heat until cooked half way through, then add the onion. Continue heating gently until the chicken has cooked through and the broth has reduced by about half. Reduce the heat to barely a simmer. Beat the eggs and pour them into the saucepan over the chicken and onion. Distribute the egg evenly then cover and cook until done (1 minute for runny eggs or 3 minutes for medium to firm).

To serve

Transfer the hot rice to a donburi bowl (or pasta bowl). Top with the egg and chicken, then garnish with spring onion or watercress, nori and shichimi according to personal taste. Enjoy with your favourite miso soup on the side. Itadakimasu!

All together NOW

Make time for conversation, coffee, comfort food and a cocktail or two at Joseph Pearce's, the bar and restaurant mingling Swedish and Scottish culture to bring all of Edinburgh together.

Joseph Pearce's, despite its very Scottish-sounding name, is actually the brainchild of Swedish couple Anna and Mike, one of eight venues in the heart of Edinburgh owned by the business partners. The couple discovered the pub in 2007 (three years after Boda, their first bar, opened on Leith Walk) just down the road from their new house. Their immediate reaction was 'this place could be amazing' but it just wasn't appealing enough to bring the neighbourhood in. The many TVs were removed, dark rooms brightened, service supercharged and a timelessly classic Swedish interior emerged to create a family-friendly place to eat and drink.

"It didn't even cross our minds to change the name," says Anna, reflecting her commitment to making people feel welcome by creating a place that's inviting enough to feel like a home from home. Anna and Mike think of their bars as 'original social networks' which provide opportunities for meeting, chatting, drinking coffee, eating comfort food, and trying fika (a Swedish concept meaning to take a small break and enjoy hot drinks with something sweet). Lots of people have met in their bars, Anna says, and their singles nights have led to

six marriages and counting! She and Mike have made great friends and love being 'matchmakers' to Edinburgh's lonely hearts. Weekends always mean the bar is buzzing, showcasing how versatile the venue is compared to its weekday draw for parents, kids and people of all ages.

Cocktails are a big part of the bar's offering, as are Champagne Sundays when people in the know come to sip their favourite luxury bubbly for very friendly prices! The selection of wines was chosen by the pair, and comfort food like Swedish meatballs alongside Scottish favourites is served through brunch, lunch and dinner. Sweden is surprisingly similar to Scotland in terms of what vegetables will grow there and the proximity of bountiful coastlines, so Joseph Pearce's aims to source locally to ensure quality and prices are to everyone's taste. Crayfish – a Swedish delicacy – have their very own celebration, though, during parties in August which are part of the bar's calendar of unique events. "If we get an idea, we run with it!" says Anna. Joseph Pearce's is the embodiment of her and Mike's optimistic attitude towards their thriving and refreshing approach to hospitality.

Joseph Pearce's
NORDIC STEW

Both Scotland and Sweden are countries with lots of coastline, so it's no wonder that we both have a fantastic range of fish soups. This Nordic stew is a combination of Swedish fish soup and Scottish cullen skink. It's perfect for cold winter days and chilly summer days too! You can also freestyle with spring vegetables when these are in season.

Preparation time: 15 minutes | Cooking time: 30 minutes | Serves: 4

Ingredients

300g salad potatoes

75g unsalted butter

2 tbsp olive oil

1 white onion, roughly diced

2 leeks, finely chopped

1 carrot, finely diced

500g smoked haddock pieces

200g smoked trout pieces

100g frozen peas

500ml milk

To finish

Handful of fresh spinach

2 spring onions, finely chopped

1 tbsp finely chopped parsley

Bread and butter, to serve

Method

Boil the potatoes in a small pan for 20 to 25 minutes until tender. Meanwhile, heat the butter and olive oil in a large pan and gently fry the onion, leeks and carrot for 10 minutes until softened. Add the haddock, trout and frozen peas. Cook on a high heat for 5 minutes, stirring gently but continuously. Then add the milk, reduce the heat and simmer for 10 minutes. Drain the potatoes and quickly cool under cold water. Cut each potato lengthways into four and add to the stew.

To finish

Add the fresh spinach and finely chopped spring onion. Serve the stew in a bowl topped with some fresh parsley; it's always best accompanied by good bread and butter.

Changing the way
YOU SEA FOOD

A boutique Scottish seafood restaurant with a social conscience, Kilted Lobster is an establishment focused on making people happy through food and community.

The ethos behind Kilted Lobster is what drives the restaurant and its social enterprise, Cooking Up A Storm. Creating exciting and satisfying food from ethically and sustainably sourced ingredients is the goal the team work towards, as well as supporting the community through a number of projects. These range from offering complimentary dining to training and work experience opportunities which provide valuable skills and get people directly into employment, as well as working with families and individuals to address dietary needs, cooking classes and budgeting.

The restaurant was opened in 2015 by chef patron Colin Hinds, following over 25 years in kitchens around the world. He returned home to Scotland and put all that experience along with his own creativity into Kilted Lobster. "I've always been working towards my own place," says Colin, "and incorporating a social conscience into that vision was always a fundamental foundation of that dream." Colin is proud of his team's entrepreneurial spirit and believes that chefs in particular are "people-pleasers" who enjoy making diners happy. This attitude extends to Cooking Up A Storm which they have even bigger plans for; 2019 should see the beginnings of a chef's academy for those who might otherwise 'slip through the net' but have the potential to start a career, using Kilted Lobster as their launch pad.

In the restaurant, up to 30 guests can enjoy freshly prepared seasonal seafood depending on availability – though lobster is, as you might expect, a mainstay of the menu! – which could come in the form of roasted langoustine, shellfish, octopus, calamari, locally caught crab, scallops from the Isle of Mull and many more delectable dishes showcasing the best that Scotland has to offer. Vegan and vegetarian options, a proudly Scottish cheeseboard and traditional desserts given contemporary twists complete the line-up.

Word of mouth has drawn most of the restaurant's visitors, since Colin and his team prefer subtlety and let their customers do the talking. Kilted Lobster has by no means gone unnoticed, however, having been crowned Best Seafood Establishment in Scotland at the Food Awards Scotland, and named in the Top Ten UK Seafood Restaurants of the Year, both in 2018. Accolades and recognition, though, play second fiddle to the restaurant's commitment to being a positive force for change, and celebrating the food its chefs love most, made with Scotland's finest produce.

Kilted Lobster
SCOTTISH SEAFOOD PLATTER FOR TWO

At Kilted Lobster, we love our mussels and greens. This wintery dish shows mussels at their best, and with the addition of garlic and seaweed this luxurious platter will boost your immune system, since it's low in fat and a great source of zinc, iron, vitamin C and B12, protein and folic acid. We're using amazing raven rock mussels from Stornoway at the moment, and we love Mara seaweed as it adds delicious flavour without having to use salt, another fantastic health benefit.

Preparation time: 15 minutes| Cooking time: 50 minutes | Serves: 2

Ingredients

1 medium-sized bulb of garlic

20ml extra-virgin olive oil

Pinch of seaweed flakes

500g langoustine

500g fresh mussels, cleaned and de-bearded

50g samphire

100g spinach

½ lemon

Salt and pepper, to taste

140g hake fillet

250g king scallop meat

Method

Preheat the oven to 180°c and slowly roast the bulb of garlic wrapped in foil for about 30 minutes, until soft and squishy. Once the garlic is cool to the touch, squeeze the gooey goodness out of the skins and mash into the olive oil and seaweed flakes.

Bring a large pot of salted water to the boil and cook the langoustine for about 4 minutes, then drain and place on the serving platter. Keeping the heat high, put the mussels into the pot with half a cup of water and the samphire. The water will steam the mussels, which should start to open, as well as the samphire. Once the mussels are half open, add the garlic oil and gently stir everything to coat evenly and ensure even cooking. Add the spinach, remove the pot from the heat and let the spinach wilt. Add a big squeeze of lemon juice, stir again and serve next to the langoustine.

Season the hake fillet then place it into a hot pan. Cook until golden on both sides, about 3 minutes each, remove from the pan and then add to the platter.

In the hot frying pan used for the hake, sear the scallops for 1 minute on each side, then place them on top of the langoustine, hake and mussels. Tuck in!

Care about
THE CAKE

Being family orientated and a place to share with your loved ones, Leo's Beanery is centred around a love for good food, flavour and creativity.

Named after Joe's grandad Leo, Marie and her husband Joe set up Leo's Beanery in 2009. Nestled between Stockbridge and Princes Street, it has become a real local's café, as well as attracting lots of tourists. They enjoy being somewhere people can stumble across and try their great coffee and delicious food.

They chose to set up in Edinburgh as they loved the beautiful city and thought all it was lacking at that time was a place that offered both good food and great coffee together, like the café scene they had left behind in Australia. They decided to take a leap of faith by opening their first business in the midst of the recession and once they'd found the venue, Joe let his creative juices flow and built everything in the café himself.

To begin with, Marie and Joe made all the food themselves too, and their combined love for cooking and food meant that it went down a storm! With their reputation growing steadily, they now have a fantastic team ensuring that every day Leo would be proud of what they all create together. Marie and Joe say that while the menus for breakfast and lunch change throughout the year "based on what we all love to eat," the menu always offers reliable favourites, and the customers really seem open to trying new things as well as enjoying the classics.

Offering fresh breakfasts, sandwiches, warming soups, hearty stews and their own take on a croque monsieur, the 'croque-mon-scones', they aim to work with small independent suppliers and producers to get the best ingredients available. The only thing not sourced locally is their coffee, and for a good reason. Rounton is a micro coffee roaster in Yorkshire, whose two founders Marie and Joe met in 2015 at the Great Taste Awards, where the café won a multitude of gold stars for several cakes. They loved them as much as their coffee and a new relationship was born.

Having expanded to more than one venue, the catering side of the business is growing too. Leo and Ted is named after Marie and Joe's grandads, continuing to show the importance of family, and caters for events across the city, so wherever you go in Edinburgh and beyond you have the chance to experience the Leo's signature passion for food, flavour and creativity.

Leo's Beanery
MINCED VENISON PIE

Leo was a lover of pies. Being from the north east of England, they were a regular sight on his table. Probably more likely to be accompanied by tinned peas and potatoes than a fresh green salad or oven roasted kale as we enjoy them, but a pie none the less! We LOVE this venison version but you can mix up the ingredients...lean minced beef and Guinness or lean minced pork and cider work exceptionally well too.

Preparation time: 15 minutes | Cooking time: 40 minutes | Serves: 4

Ingredients

For the pastry:

400g plain flour

200g unsalted butter

2 large eggs, beaten

1 large egg, beaten separately (for the egg wash)

For the filling:

100g (about 4) shallots, finely diced

1 large carrot, finely diced

1 large stick of celery, finely diced

1 large clove of garlic, finely diced or grated

600g lean venison mince

8 juniper berries, crushed (optional)

2 tsp fresh rosemary, finely chopped

2 tsp fresh thyme, finely chopped

250ml dark ale

250ml vegetable stock

3 tsp cornflour, mixed with 10ml cold water

Salt and pepper

Method

For the pastry

Rub the butter and flour together to a fine breadcrumb consistency then add the two beaten eggs and mix until a dough is formed. Press together with your hands and place in the fridge for at least 20 minutes.

For the filling

Brown off the shallots, carrots and celery gently in a large frying pan for 5 minutes before adding the garlic to cook for a further 2 minutes. Set aside in a bowl, leaving the pan on the heat. Brown off the venison mince, cooking gently for 3 to 5 minutes, ensuring the moisture is retained. Return the vegetables to the pan along with the crushed juniper berries, chopped herbs, ale and vegetable stock. Lastly, add the cornflour paste to the pan, stir well and bring to a simmer. Leave for approximately 10 minutes or until thickened then season to taste.

To assemble and cook the pie

Preheat the oven to 180°c. Place the chilled pastry on a floured surface and cut in half. Roll one half out to 2mm thickness and line a greased pie tin with it. Trim off excess pastry from around the edges. Prepare the other half in the same way to make the pie lid. Feel free to make shapes or letters with your excess pastry!

Transfer the filling into the pastry case and brush the edges with egg wash before laying the pastry lid on top. Pinch along the edges to seal before trimming again, then brush the top with more egg wash. Place the pie into the preheated oven for 25 to 30 minutes, or until pastry is golden and the filling is piping hot. Slice, serve and enjoy!

A roaring
GOOD TIME

One stylish bar and bistro has brought a new lease of life to a forgotten corner of Leith through cracking cocktails, gourmet burgers and good vibes till late.

Built on the bones of one of Edinburgh's most infamous pubs, The Lioness of Leith has brought locals a bar and bistro that welcomes everyone from late night revellers to families and dog owners alike. Owners Ben Abbot and Danny Zyw have brought an ethos of inclusivity and a focus on great drinks and proper food to the venture. Ben moved back home from London, discovered the derelict pub on Duke Street and worked on its renovation for nearly a year with Danny, completing over 90 percent of the work themselves. The labour of love paid off when The Lioness opened its doors just before Christmas 2013. People really took to its combination of good food and eclectic funky décor, while the cocktails were an instant hit, with choices from the extensive selection of inventive mixes and inspired local takes on the classics, like Sunshine on Leith and Nae Cream-a Colada.

In early 2018 the pair reinvented the bistro side of the business, a new gourmet burger menu was launched and 'Lioness Burgers' was born. Head chef and burger enthusiast Brad Charters was brought in to spearhead the culinary change. Lioness Burgers sets itself apart through the incredibly high standards met by the food from farm to fork; beef is sourced from award-winning local butcher Findlay's of Portobello and the chicken is all free-range, slow-grown and herb-fed. The artisan burger buns are baked under a mile away, including gluten-free options so no one misses out. To this end, there are always at least four meat-free burgers on the menu, offering both vegetarians and vegans a move away from the usual 'token' choices.

It's important to Ben, Danny, Brad and the whole management team that the food, drink and atmosphere create a joyful experience for the customer. This desire to host happy occasions has grown to incorporate outside events, which the team can cater for with both cocktails and food as well as private parties within the venue. With the local area experiencing a renaissance – TimeOut magazine voted Leith in the top 25 coolest neighbourhoods in the world in September 2018 – The Lioness of Leith and Lioness Burgers are set to continue writing over the building's 'dark history' with their own brand of innovative, honest, ethical and locally made food, drinks and good times.

The Lioness of Leith
THE MOUNT FUJI BURGER

This burger went on the restaurant menu as a special but quickly became a firm favourite amongst staff and customers. Best served with an ice-cold citrus ale of your choosing.

Preparation time: 15 minutes, plus a minimum of 3 hours pickling | Cooking time: 10 minutes | Serves: 4

Ingredients

750g beef mince (we like a 70/30 meat to fat ratio) using cuts of your choosing

150g gluten-free flour

50g plain flour

350ml soda or sparkling water

1 large kohlrabi

1 cucumber

2 large red finger chillies

300ml rice wine vinegar

4 tbsp caster sugar

Salt and pepper, to taste

400ml teriyaki sauce

4 brioche buns

50g salted butter

2 tbsp black sesame seeds

2 tbsp sesame seeds

2 spring onions

Method

First prepare all the ingredients. Divide the beef mince into four equal balls. Add both flours to a bowl, mix with the soda or sparkling water to form a batter and then set aside. Peel and thinly slice the kohlrabi and then chop into matchsticks.

To make the cucumber pickle, use a peeler to create thin ribbons of cucumber, discarding the watery centre where all the seeds are. Thinly slice the chillies and add them to the cucumber in a bowl. Mix the rice wine vinegar and caster sugar until all sugar has dissolved, then pour the pickling liquor over the cucumber and chillies. Leave for 24 hours for best results, or 2 to 3 hours as a minimum.

Heat a griddle pan to a high temperature. Flatten the balls of beef into burger shapes, lightly season with salt and pepper and place them on the griddle pan. While the burgers are grilling, dip the kohlrabi matchsticks in the batter prepared earlier and then deep fry them at 180°c for 3 minutes. Drain the kohlrabi and set aside. Turn the burgers after 4 minutes and coat the sealed side with teriyaki sauce using a brush. Cook the burgers for a further 3 to 4 minutes.

To assemble the burgers, first slice the brioche buns in half and place a small knob of butter on each half. Toast the buns in a dry pan on a medium heat until golden and then lightly brush each cut side with teriyaki sauce. Place some of the pickled cucumber on the bottom half of each bun. Remove the burgers from the griddle pan and liberally glaze both sides with teriyaki sauce before placing them onto the buns. Top each with some tempura kohlrabi. Combine both types of sesame seeds and sprinkle a little over the burger and tempura kohlrabi. Thinly slice the spring onion and sprinkle over then finish the burgers by putting the 'lid' of the bun on top.

From farm TO FORK

At the heart of a family farm, Loch Leven's Larder is a haven for fresh produce and wholesome food that puts great veg and fantastic service centre stage.

Emma and Rob Niven founded Loch Leven's Larder in 2005, after moving to the area with a desire to champion local produce. They are the third generation to farm their land, which stretches over 1000 acres and overlooks – as the name suggests – the beautiful Loch Leven. As a couple with young kids, finding really nice places to eat good healthy food was important, so when few presented themselves Emma and Rob decided to establish their own for the area's benefit, and to keep their farm's produce from being shipped away and enjoyed elsewhere.

"From there, everything just snowballed" as they put it, and Loch Leven's Larder is now a thriving business comprising a food hall, two cafés, and a tasting room where classes from bread making to skincare and evening events are held. Within the food hall there is a butchery, run and stocked by a local butcher, a deli with a huge selection of British, Scottish and international cheeses, and a purpose-built bakery which is the source of all the fresh bread at the Larder as well as quiches, pies, sausage rolls and much more. The open, bright, contemporary space was enhanced by a recent extension, rendering the black timbered building even more beautiful and unique while making the most of its stunning views across the loch and farmland.

The entire business is founded on a drive to create change, by celebrating the hospitality industry as one worthy of respect and enthusiasm, and convincing people that vegetables can be sexy! Emma describes her ethos as "driven by great service, provenance, and sourcing produce locally" which means they work very seasonally and offer wholesome food in all aspects of the Larder. The café menus reflect what's growing on the farm, with table service space for 120 as well as 'The Greenhouse' which provides friendly yet speedy service for active customers fresh from a park run or cycle ride around the loch.

Having become one of the largest employers in the area, the Larder's founders cite their staff as "the real strength of the business." In 2018, they proudly added the title of Perthshire Chamber of Commerce's Independent Retailer to a host of awards, and look forward to more farming, more veg and more happy customers in future.

Loch Leven's Larder
BRUSSELS SPROUT SALAD WITH CHESTNUTS & SMOKED PANCETTA

This recipe was created by head chef Brian Padmore at Loch Leven's Larder and is an excellent winter starter or main.

Preparation time: 5 minutes | Cooking time: 15 minutes | Serves: 4-6

Ingredients

Pinch of salt

500g brussels sprouts

200g cavolo nero (black kale)

200g smoked pancetta lardons

200g tinned chestnuts, drained

50g unsalted butter

1 sprig of rosemary, leaves stripped from the stem

1 lemon, zested

To serve (optional):

Crumbled goat's cheese

Pomegranate seeds

Method

Add a pinch of salt and 2 litres of water to a large saucepan, and heat to a rolling boil. Meanwhile, peel the sprouts and use a sharp knife to make a shallow 'x' across the bottom of each one. Blanch the sprouts for 2 to 3 minutes, then remove and plunge into cold water. Drain the sprouts then cut them in half and set aside.

Tear the leaves from the stalks of the cavolo nero and roughly chop them. Blanch in the boiling water for 1 minute, drain and then press out any remaining water using a cloth.

In a large saucepan, gently fry the lardons on a low heat until the fat has melted and the lardons are dark and crispy. Remove and discard about half of the fat. Take the lardons out of the pan (leaving the remaining fat in) and spread them out on a paper towel to absorb any fat.

Turn the heat up to medium and add the drained sprouts to the fat. Stir gently for 2 to 3 minutes to ensure the sprouts are cooked evenly. Add the chestnuts and fry for another 1 to 1½ minutes. Add the butter, cavolo nero, rosemary leaves and grated lemon zest then cook for another minute. Add the cooked lardons then give everything a good mix before serving.

To serve

This dish works well as a side for your Christmas lunch but can also be enjoyed as a warm winter salad, ideally with a sprinkle of crumbled goat's cheese and pomegranate seeds scattered over the top. For a vegetarian option, omit the pancetta and fry in olive oil.

Muscle in for some shellfish
INDULGENCE!

In the heart of the buzzing city centre, Mussel Inn is the place to go for all manner of mouth-watering seafood fresh from Scottish waters.

Award-winning Scottish seafood restaurant Mussel Inn was founded on Edinburgh's Rose Street 20 years ago by a mussel farmer and a scallop farmer. They decided to buck the trend of Scottish shellfish being immediately exported to the continent by making it available in Scotland in their very own restaurant. Mussel Inn is now renowned for its delicious locally sourced fresh seafood as well as meat and vegetarian dishes, providing excellent value for money and quick and friendly service. It's headed up by Swede Janne Johansson with his sons Matt and Kristian, whose direct close contact with their shellfish farmer associates ensures they receive the best quality produce available at any given time.

When Mussel Inn first opened, not many diners ate mussels and it played a pioneering role in helping to introduce shellfish into the mainstream Scottish diet. Its mussels are grown on ropes in sea lochs on the west of Scotland and the Shetland Isles. The mussels feed naturally in the plankton-rich waters; sustainability and caring for the environment are of utmost importance to their growers.

Despite its name, the restaurant offers much more to diners than just mussels. While they remain a popular staple, the menu now includes a broader selection of fresh Scottish seafood dishes than ever before. Grilled queenies; piri piri tiger prawns; crab salad; queen scallops; sea bass; tiger prawns; pan fried king scallops; chargrilled scallops; shellfish pasta and chilled or grilled oysters are just a few of the delicacies available!

Its sustainably cultivated oysters, nurtured in the cold, clear sea lochs of the west coast, grow more slowly than those from warmer waters, providing a richness and depth of taste that is unique. Mussel Inn's outside seating area – offering diners the opportunity to enjoy a platter of oysters or a pot of mussels al fresco while people-watching, beside the fully pedestrianised Rose Street in the heart of Edinburgh's New Town – is always a popular option, and The Mussel Inn also offers special two and three course pre-theatre menus. The 'lunchtime quickies' offer diners a selection of healthy and nutritious freshly prepared dishes, and there's a varied daily specials board too, featuring dishes carefully prepared by the team of chefs and chosen daily from selected suppliers.

Mussel Inn
GRILLED QUEEN SCALLOPS WITH BLACK PUDDING AND YELLOW PEPPER DRESSING

This appetising starter has a delicious, full flavour featuring delectably sweet and juicy queenies at its heart.

Preparation time: 10 minutes | Cooking time: 15 minutes | Serves: 4

Ingredients

12 wafer-thin slices of black pudding

24 queen scallops, cleaned

Olive oil

Salt and pepper

Micro herbs (such as red basil and rocket)

8 cherry tomatoes, quartered

16 viola petals

For the yellow pepper dressing:

1 yellow pepper, finely diced

100g Spanish onion, finely chopped

2 cloves of garlic, peeled

150ml olive oil

200ml vegetable stock

Pinch of sugar

Pinch of turmeric

2 tbsp vinegar

Salt and pepper, to taste

Method

For the yellow pepper dressing

In a large frying pan, sauté the yellow peppers, onion and garlic with a little olive oil over a medium heat for 2 to 3 minutes. Add the vegetable stock to the pan with the sugar and turmeric, and continue to cook until most of the liquid has gone. Add the mix to a food processor and blend to a smooth purée, add the vinegar and remaining olive oil and blend again until combined. Strain through a fine sieve, season to taste then set aside until needed.

Place the sliced black pudding under the grill on a low heat and cook for 4 to 5 minutes, turning every couple of minutes until dark and crispy. Leave on kitchen paper to drain.

Preheat the grill to its hottest setting and place the queen scallops on a tray. Drizzle with some olive oil and season them then place under the grill. They only take a couple of minutes to cook so plate up during this time then serve the scallops hot.

To serve

Arrange three slices of black pudding on the centre of each plate. Drizzle the yellow pepper dressing around the plate, scatter over the micro herbs, add four quarters of cherry tomatoes and some viola petals over the dish. Finish with the scallops straight from the grill.

Mussel Inn
MOROCCAN STEAMED MUSSELS WITH COCONUT MILK

A generous sprinkling of chillies and spices make this aromatic dish a taste of Africa mixed with the best Scottish mussels, for diners keen to spice up their dinner a little!

Preparation time: 10 minutes | Cooking time: 6-8 minutes | Serves: 4

Ingredients

3 whole red chillies

3 whole green chillies

1 small onion, finely chopped

1 tbsp brown mustard seeds

3 cloves of garlic, finely chopped

20g fresh ginger, finely chopped

80ml olive oil

½ tsp ground cumin

¼ tsp ground coriander

½ tsp paprika

¼ tsp turmeric

¼ tsp ground nutmeg

2kg mussels, cleaned

125ml dry white wine

150ml coconut milk

Small bunch of coriander, chopped

Salt and pepper, to taste

3 spring onions, finely sliced

Method

To make the Moroccan base, cut the chillies in half lengthways, remove the stalks, carefully scrape out all the seeds and discard them, cut out any white membrane from the centre of each chilli, slice each piece of chilli into strips, bunch the strips together and cut across them to dice. If you want maximum heat from the chillies leave the seeds and white membrane in.

Put the diced chillies into a small container and add the onion, mustard seeds, garlic, fresh ginger, olive oil and all the spices. This is best done the day before and left covered in the fridge, so all those wonderful flavours can infuse slowly.

Place a large pan on a high heat with some olive oil and add four tablespoons of the Moroccan mix (being careful not to burn it) with the mussels and white wine. Cover and cook for 3 minutes, shaking or stirring occasionally. Once the mussels start to open, add the coconut milk and cover the pan again. Continue cooking for a further 2 minutes or until the coconut milk starts to bubble. Add some of the chopped coriander (reserve some for garnish) and give everything a good stir. Taste and season with salt and pepper.

To serve

Ladle the mussels into warm bowls with plenty of the Moroccan coconut milk sauce. Discard any mussels that have failed to open. Garnish the dishes with spring onions and the reserved coriander.

Scott by name, Scot by NATURE

Dining at The Newport means being treated to Scottish produce in all its glory, cooked by passionate chefs who aim to reflect the quality and beauty of their surroundings.

Sitting on the banks of the River Tay and offering views through panoramic windows over the restaurant's two floors, The Newport is a beautifully converted former hotel and includes four individually designed rooms. General manager Jonny has the practical side of the venue in hand, putting the stylish contemporary interiors on a par with the modern take on classical style in the cooking. There is also an adjacent bar under refurbishment to form a lounge and drinking area which will complete the overall dining experience.

The atmosphere draws people to its door too; the dining space can seat 50 people and feels vibrant yet relaxed, buzzing with excitement over the food which the chefs themselves often bring out, leading to lots of interaction between guests and staff that showcases the food all the better. With fish, meat, dairy, vegetables and more from Fife and beyond – right up to each coast, out to the Hebrides and other islands, and down to the border – on the à la carte and tasting menus, chef patron Jamie Scott celebrates Scotland's finest produce as well as his area's thriving food scene.

"There's so much quality here. Producers, farmers, growers and independent places like us form strong bonds; there's no competition which makes sourcing fantastic ingredients very easy and a joy to do," he says.

Since opening in 2016, the restaurant has developed through Jamie's careful attention to detail. His team includes recently promoted head chef, Tasso, a "driving force in the kitchen" and his sous chef Shaz who is, again in Jamie's words, an "absolute hero" for her commitment and hard work. He also credits his wife Kelly with working tirelessly behind the scenes at The Newport, before and after their twin daughters were born in 2018! Jamie oversees his team and shapes the food according to "who's got what at the time" – referring to his exclusively Scottish suppliers – as well as Thai and Indian influences from his own interests.

The whole team were incredibly proud to be awarded Restaurant of the Year for 2018-19 by the AA. Being young and hungry for success has been balanced by insights they've gained along the way, resulting in "the best cooking they've done so far" and sights firmly set on where they want to be in years to come.

The Newport

CURED SEA TROUT, PEAR, BURNT LEMON AND RYE SAUCE

"The dish started in the summer with the wild variety of trout, but we still have it on the menu for which we are using the amazing Loch Etive trout. The marriage of the oil-rich fish works brilliantly with the tangy rye sauce and very citric lemon purée."

Preparation time: 15 minutes, plus 5 hours curing | Cooking time: approximately 45 minutes | Serves: 4

Ingredients

For the trout:

1 side of sea trout, skinned and pin-boned

200g coarse sea salt

100g fine salt

500g caster sugar

3 juniper berries

100g dill

For the rye sauce:

1 shallot, peeled and sliced

2 cloves of garlic, peeled and sliced

2 tsbp vegetable oil

50g white leek, washed and sliced

50g celery, washed and sliced

250ml rye beer

250ml fish stock

100ml double cream

1 tbsp crème fraîche

Salt and pepper

Squeeze of lemon juice

For the lemon purée:

6 lemons

100g caster sugar

400ml water

For the garnish:

2 pears, 1 cut julienne and 1 with a parisienne scoop

4 walnuts, peeled and broken up

4 tsp keta salmon caviar

Few sprigs of sea purslane

Method

For the trout

Rinse the sea trout to ensure there are no scales or bones. Blend the remaining ingredients together until the dill is incorporated. Completely cover the fish in the cure and leave for 5 hours. Thoroughly rinse the fish under cold water, cut into even 3 by 10cm rectangles and set aside.

For the rye sauce

Gently sweat the shallot and garlic in a saucepan with the oil. Add the leek and celery and continue to cook until soft. Add the beer and increase the heat. Reduce the liquid by two thirds and then repeat the process with the fish stock then the cream. Pass the sauce through a fine sieve and whisk in the crème fraîche. Season with salt, pepper and lemon juice. Keep warm until serving.

For the lemon purée

Pierce the lemons all over with a sharp knife. Blanch in boiling water for 20 seconds then plunge into iced water. Repeat this five more times to remove the bitterness from the lemons. Heat the sugar and water in a saucepan to get a dark caramel, add the lemons and carefully crush. Add another 200ml of water and boil for 8 to 12 minutes. Blend until smooth, pass through a sieve and place into a piping bag.

To serve

Rub the trout fillets with a little oil then char with a blowtorch. To plate, spoon some of the rye sauce into the middle of the serving bowl. Place the fish in the centre; add six dots of lemon purée, six pieces of each pear (the julienne and parisienne cuts) and some walnut pieces. Finish with a spoonful of the caviar and the purslane leaves.

The Newport

48-HOUR BEEF SHORT RIB, BIRCH GLAZED SWEETBREAD, CARROT & PARSLEY

"We always have a beef rib dish on the menu and this has been our favourite variation. The smoky rib works amazingly well in contrast with the sticky sweetbread, the carrots are cooked in the liquor that eventually becomes the sauce and the parsley just freshens everything up beautifully."

Preparation time: 30 minutes, plus 3 hours for the short rib | Cooking time: 20 minutes, plus 48 hours for the short rib | Serves: 4

Ingredients

For the short rib:

1.4kg short rib, bones and skin removed

2 shallots, peeled and sliced

200g beef fat

Few sprigs of thyme

Wild watercress, to garnish

For the parsley purée:

8 shallots

100g butter

100ml white chicken stock

250g parsley leaves (no stalks)

100ml double cream

For the pickled and braised carrot:

100ml white wine vinegar

200ml sugar

1 tsp pink peppercorns

3 large carrots

50ml vegetable oil

500ml dark veal stock

100ml Concord vinegar

For the sweetbread:

250g rose sweetbreads, trimmed and sinew removed

25g plain flour, seasoned

50g butter

100ml birch or maple syrup

Method

For the short rib

Blowtorch the trimmed meat all over to give a nice charred flavour. Cook the shallots in the beef fat with the thyme. Cool then place the short rib and shallots into a vacuum pack bag and seal. Cook at 56°c for 48 hours in a water bath. Once cooked remove from the bag and discard the shallots and thyme. Press the meat between two trays with weight on top for 2 to 3 hours until cooled completely. Trim away the edges and cut into 4cm by 12cm rectangles.

For the parsley purée

Cook the shallots in the butter on a low heat until soft, then add the stock and parsley and cook for a further 2 to 3 minutes. Blend in a food processor, adding a touch of the cream, until smooth then season to taste. Pass the purée through a sieve into a piping bag.

For the pickled and braised carrot

Combine 100ml of water with the vinegar, sugar and peppercorns in a saucepan, then bring to the boil. Allow to cool slightly while you peel and slice one of the carrots into 1cm rounds. Add the sliced carrot to the pickling liquor.

Heat the oil in a heavy-bottomed saucepan, peel the remaining two whole carrots then colour them all over in the pan. Once golden, add the veal stock. Cook until the carrots are tender.

Remove the carrots and reduce the remaining stock until a sauce consistency is achieved. Season with salt and the Concord vinegar, then pass through a chinois.

For the sweetbread

Dredge the sweetbreads in the seasoned flour, heat a tablespoon of olive oil in a frying pan until hot, add the sweetbread and cook until crisp and golden for about 3 minutes. Turn over and cook for a further 2 minutes then add the butter and syrup. Cook until reduced and sticky. Remove from the pan and rest for 5 minutes. Slice each piece into four just before serving.

To assemble

Place a spoonful of the purée in the centre of the plate and flatten out. Place the short rib in the centre, add the sweetbread, braised carrots and pickled carrot, then finish with the sauce and some wild watercress.

The Newport
TAGH MI SUAS (TIRAMISU)

"We really wanted to showcase a couple of Scottish ingredients: coffee from Arbroath, the awesome Katy Rodger's crowdie cheese and chocolate from Chocolate Tree in Edinburgh. The natural flavour combinations gave us our take on the classic Italian tiramisu."

Preparation time: 20 minutes, plus 1 hour 30 minutes setting | Cooking time: 10 minutes | Serves: 4

Ingredients

For the cocoa sponge:

5 eggs

115g icing sugar

125g cocoa powder

For the coffee jelly:

4 shots of espresso

50g caster sugar

1½ sheets of gelatine, soaked in water

For the chocolate mousse:

225g 70% chocolate

375ml double cream

185g caster sugar

5 yolks and 2 whole eggs

20ml Drambuie

For the mirror glaze:

300g sugar

100g cocoa powder

250ml double cream

6 sheets of gelatine, soaked in water

For the crowdie mousse:

600g crowdie cheese

40g egg yolks

3 eggs

100g sugar

200ml cream

Method

For the cocoa sponge

Whisk the eggs and icing sugar together using an electric mixer until thick, pale and creamy. Gently fold the cocoa powder in then spread the mixture onto a lined baking sheet into a 2cm thick layer. Bake at 180°c for 6 to 8 minutes, allow to cool, then cut 4cm discs out of the sponge using a ring cutter.

For the coffee jelly

Bring the espresso, sugar and 100ml of water to the boil then remove from the heat. Add the soaked gelatine and stir to dissolve. Pass the mixture through a sieve then pour into small chocolate moulds or ice cube trays. Leave in the freezer to set.

For the chocolate mousse

Melt the chocolate in a bain-marie while whisking the cream to soft peaks. Heat the sugar and 75ml of water to 121°c in a small pan. Whisk the eggs and yolks until pale and creamy then slowly add the hot sugar syrup. Whisk until cold, fold the chocolate into the egg mixture, add the cream and mix gently until incorporated. Pipe the mousse into lined moulds (5cm dariole moulds or similar) so they are one third full, then press a coffee jelly into the centre, and fill almost to the top with mousse. Smooth the surface and tap the mould to get rid of air bubbles, place a disc of chocolate sponge on top, brush with a little of the Drambuie and then place in the freezer for 1 hour to set.

For the mirror glaze

Bring the sugar and 240ml of water to the boil, add the cocoa powder and boil again. Repeat with the cream then remove from the heat and add the soaked gelatine. Pour into a deep but narrow container and leave to cool to 35°c.

For the crowdie mousse

In a bain-marie, whisk the crowdie, yolks, eggs and sugar until smooth, then add the cream and heat to 60°c. Pass the mixture through a sieve and straight into a cream whipper. Charge twice and leave at room temperature. If you don't have a cream whipper, simply whisk the mousse by hand to soft peak stage.

To assemble

Remove the layered mousse, jelly and sponge from the freezer and pierce the centre about half way down using a long skewer. Dip it into the mirror glaze, not submerging the sponge fully, then place on a wire rack and leave for 5 to 6 minutes to set. To serve, sit the glazed mousse just off centre on the plate and finish with a spoonful of crowdie mousse on the side.

From Port
TO PLATE

North Port celebrates Scottish produce by refining the flavours derived from its landscape, and serving them in a friendly, casual, welcoming restaurant overlooking the River Tay.

North Port is a restaurant created and run by Andrew, a chef, and his wife Karen, the front of house manager, to showcase the carefully selected ingredients they source from local growers, breeders, suppliers and foragers. They opened in 2014 after having searched high and low in Scotland for the perfect venue and location, which they discovered in Perth at the beautiful old building now housing their first venture. "It's a pretty unique space," says Andrew, "and still a work in progress as we are always aiming to improve our food and the restaurant in general."

Running their own restaurant has given Andrew and Karen the creative freedom they wanted, resulting in dishes that present "the best ingredients in the world" – mostly sourced from Perthshire, famed for its fantastic produce and passionately advocated by Andrew – in a way that makes the most of their flavours without over-complicating them. The emphasis on local meat, game, dairy and vegetables even extends to foraging, done by Andrew and the team down the banks of the River Tay which is right on their doorstep.

This ethos doesn't stop with the food either; Scottish beers populate the bar, and there's even a selection of artisanal mead which is created nearby using natural botanicals. This same approach has been adopted by the whole team, who recently embarked on distilling their own gin, made by combining four or five wild hand-picked ingredients to create small batches at the local distillery which already supplies the restaurant.

North Port's beautifully presented, refined and inventive food has already earned it a spot in the Good Food Guide three years running. They've also just received a second rosette, but for Andrew and Karen, ensuring guests enjoy what they do is more important than any accolades. The restaurant's welcoming atmosphere contributes to this goal, enhanced by features such as wood panelling which keeps the dining rooms cosy during the evening and bright during the day. Tables are well spaced to offer guests an intimate experience, which reflects the precision and care taken with flavours on the plate. Friendly, relaxed service sets the scene for a casual meal out, while special occasion dining in the private Tay Room can be tailored to any tastes. "Everyone working here gets what we're about in terms of both food and service," says Andrew, "so we share a commitment to the guests that runs through everything we do."

North Port
BEETROOT, YOGHURT, DILL, MUSTARD SEEDS

Beetroot is such a versatile and delicious vegetable. This dish is a great example of what we do at the restaurant by bringing out the best in individual ingredients and not overcomplicating flavours.

Preparation time: 48 hours | Cooking time: 8 hours | Serves: 4

Ingredients

25g yoghurt

For the pickling liquor:

100ml each of cider vinegar and white wine

100g caster sugar

2 bay leaves

1 tbsp each of fennel and mustard seeds

For the roasted beetroot:

1 large golden beetroot

2 large purple beetroot

6 sprigs of thyme

For the beetroot tartare:

1 large candy beetroot

Rapeseed oil, salt and cider vinegar

For the beetroot meringue:

30g egg whites

½ tsp cider vinegar

12g maltodextrin

15g beetroot powder

¼ tsp xanthan

For the beetroot sauce:

1 medium golden beetroot

¼ tsp xanthan

For the pickled mustard seeds:

100ml cider vinegar

50ml dark ale

25g brown sugar

100g mustard seeds

Method

For the pickling liquor

Place all the ingredients in a saucepan with 150ml of water and bring to the boil. Take off the heat and allow to cool.

For the roasted beetroot

Do this 2 days in advance of serving the dish. Rub the beetroot with rapeseed oil and season with salt, then wrap in tin foil with the thyme, keeping the two types of beetroot separate. Bake in an oven at 150°c for around 7 hours until soft. Allow the beetroot to cool in the foil, then peel and scoop pieces out using a melon baller. Place the purple beetroot in the pickling liquor and store in the fridge for at least 48 hours before using.

For the beetroot tartare

Peel and finely dice the beetroot , reserving four large slices for the discs. Season to taste with the oil, salt and vinegar.

For the beetroot meringue

Whip the egg whites and vinegar to soft peaks. Add the remaining ingredients and a pinch of salt and continue to whip. Spread thinly onto a silicon mat and dry out in an oven at 70°c.

For the beetroot sauce

Peel and roughly chop the beetroot then blitz in a food processor with 50ml of water. Pass the liquid through muslin into a bowl, then whisk in the xanthan to slightly thicken the juice. Season with salt.

For the pickled mustard seeds

Add all the ingredients except the mustard seeds to the pan and simmer. Once the sugar has dissolved, add the seeds. Gently simmer for around 30 to 45 minutes until the liquid has thickened and the seeds have plumped up.

To assemble

In a wide bowl, make a ring with the candy beetroot tartare leaving a space in the middle. Add some of the pickled beetroot and roasted golden beetroot on top of the tartare, then small spoonfuls of the mustard seeds and the yoghurt. Garnish with the meringue and sprigs of dill. Transfer about 10 to 15ml of the beetroot sauce per person to a small jug. To serve, pour the sauce into the gap in the centre of the plate.

The Gin-Credible Taste
OF BOMBAY

Pickering's Gin is 'botanically engineered' by Marcus Pickering, Matthew Gammell and their team at Summerhall Distillery, the product of many years of friendship and some crafty DIY...

Marcus and Matt, the founders of Pickering's Gin, have been business partners for more than 14 years and friends for even longer. They ran a property management company together, which was commissioned by Robert McDowell, owner of Summerhall, to renovate the old Vet School he had just purchased. Keen for the challenge, Marcus and Matt agreed, and the conversion of the dilapidated venue into event spaces and a pub created a successful arts community.

The story of Pickering's Gin itself began when a gin recipe titled "Mount Mary, Bombay 1947" arrived on Marcus' desk; a handwritten piece of India's history sent by a friend which became the distillery's raison d'être. After months of fine-tuning, the ambitious pair created a classic dry gin that laid the foundation for the unique range of products that followed. In their first year, they released a 57.1% Navy Strength Gin in collaboration with the Royal Edinburgh Military Tattoo (which boasts a bearskin hat on every bottle!), and a year after that saw the release of the 70 year-old Bombay recipe: Pickering's 1947 Original Recipe Gin.

Whisky lovers shouldn't miss out on Pickering's Oak Aged Collection; Marcus and Matt have captured incredible tasting notes of whisky-soaked oak across five of Scotland's whisky regions in their gin. A sloe gin and the wildly popular 'gin baubles' complete the line up so far, with a tipple for every season and occasion.

Believe it or not, the initial idea was intended to meet only Matt's and Marcus' gin needs, perhaps extending to family and friends at most. However, when the Edinburgh press discovered the city's first gin distillery in 150 years, things took a different track, turning their hobby into a flourishing business. As creative handymen and engineers, they built their own distillery using household heating elements to power their innovative bain-marie distilling system. The old Royal Vet School became the birthplace of their award-winning creations, all of which are modernised, tinkered with, aged, distilled, bottled, labelled and waxed in-house. Within only a few years Pickering's Gin has become the gin of choice amongst Edinburgh's acclaimed establishments. The modern variations on classic Bombay style have even made it across Europe, New Zealand, Australia, China, Hong Kong, and the United States, but Pickering's remains a proudly Scottish gin (with a dash of exotic heritage) through and through.

Pickering's Gin
SHRUB THE DECKS

"I've nodded to our Navy Strength Gin by creating a shrub using fresh lime, which everyone once knew and loved as the classic go-to garnish for a G&T. I've paired this with stem ginger, which sublimely complements the spiced botanicals from our original Bombay recipe. Agave nectar seamlessly binds the powerful 57.1% gin with the tart and sweet notes of the shrub, and cloudy apple juice lengthens the serve into a long, spiced and citrussy sip."
Stevie Watson, Global Brand Ambassador

Preparation time: 5 minutes, plus 1 week for the shrub | Serves: 1

Ingredients

For the shrub:

4 limes

8 heaped tsp freshly grated ginger

220g Demerara sugar

450ml apple cider vinegar

For the cocktail:

40ml Pickering's Navy Strength Gin 57.1%

25ml stem ginger and fresh lime shrub

20ml agave nectar

20ml cloudy apple juice

15ml fresh lime juice

25ml soda water

2 dashes of lemon bitters

Method

For the shrub

Zest all the limes then cut them into quarters. Combine the zest, lime quarters, fresh ginger and sugar in a non-metal bowl. Cover and set aside somewhere cool (not cold) for 2 days. Strain the mixture, reserving the liquid, then muddle the limes to get the rest of the juice from them and stir back into the liquid. Leave for another 3 hours, stir again then discard the limes. Stir in the vinegar and pour through a funnel into sterilised bottles. Seal tightly, store in the fridge and shake every day to help dissolve the rest of the sugar.

For the cocktail

Add all of the ingredients to a cocktail shaker and shake hard for 15 seconds until the shaker is frosted.

To serve

Fill a highball glass with crushed ice and pour in the cocktail. Add more crushed ice if necessary and top with a splash of soda water as you would a classic Collins. Garnish with a classic lime wheel and rosemary sprig.

Eyes on THE PIES

Pie Not has developed on the strength of chef Stephen Lindsay's love for great ingredients and his dedication to the venture, transforming a one-man band into a thriving neighbourhood bistro.

Stephen Lindsay has been a chef since the age of 16, and started Pie Not by making everything himself from scratch, in a bid to bring a high standard of artisan pies to Edinburgh. From selling at markets to supplying local businesses, the venture grew naturally thanks to the quality of the food and the passion Stephen put into his work every day. The goal had always been to open his own place, so when opportunity came knocking in October 2017, just a few weeks of refurbishments stood between him and The Pie Not? Bistro.

Emma came on board to drive sales and, with a background in catering, is now a partner in the business. With help from their families and friends they have started a quiet pie revolution, and have seen huge popularity with locals as well as national acclaim in the British Pie Awards, at which Pie Not has scooped medals every year since 2015. Stephen is still just where he wants to be though, with lots of time spent in the kitchen heading up the team.

The bistro is committed to sustainability, provenance, and of course keeping everything locally sourced where possible. The flour is locally grown and milled in East Lothian, the butter is Scottish and the meat, fruit and vegetables are fresh and delivered daily from suppliers. Pies are weighed, pressed, filled, and cooked by hand and all the baking is done on site; the bistro revolves around really fresh, simple food done well. As well as the star attraction, there are specials, starters, puddings and breakfasts on the menu, plus coffee and freshly baked sweet treats to make sure Pie Not is a place for everyone, any time of day.

Being situated in a residential area, the Pie Not team hugely value their many regular customers as well as the network of other independents they have built strong friendships with. "It's all about community; we work a lot with the school across the road, the older demographic, our nearby church… everyone has a warm welcome at the bistro," says Emma. "We love to support our neighbours, and people are rooting for us which is such a great feeling."

The Pie Not? Bistro
CLASSIC FISH PIE

This is a simple but extremely tasty pie. It means a lot to us because it was our first gold medal winner at the British Pie Awards back in 2015. You can double the filling to freeze in portions, and that way you have quick and nutritious meals ready for the whole family.

Preparation time: 20 minutes | Cooking time: 45 minutes | Serves: 4-6

Ingredients

For the pastry:

225g plain flour

100g salted butter, diced

60ml cold water

For the filling:

1kg Maris Piper or Rooster potatoes, peeled and chopped

Splash of milk

Knob of butter

Freshly ground black pepper

400g mixed fish (we use salmon, smoked haddock and cod)

25g butter

25g plain flour

4 spring onions, finely chopped

400ml milk

Handful of frozen peas

200g grated cheddar

1 egg, beaten

Method

For the pastry

As pie makers, we would obviously suggest making your own pastry! However, you can pick up some ready-made pastry at your local supermarket if preferred.

Sift the flour into a large bowl, add all the butter and rub in with your fingertips until the mixture resembles fine breadcrumbs. Add the water and mix. Tip out onto a floured surface and work gently until the pastry comes together. Flatten the ball slightly, dust with flour then set aside. Do not chill.

For the filling

Preheat the oven to 200°c and get six individual (11cm diameter) foil pie dishes ready. These are easy to find online or from Lakeland.

Put all the potatoes into a saucepan and pour over enough water to cover them. Bring to the boil then simmer until tender. When cooked, drain thoroughly and mash with the splash of milk and knob of butter. Season with black pepper to taste.

Place the fish in a medium-sized pan, cover with cold water and bring to the boil, then reduce the temperature and simmer for 10 minutes until cooked. Drain the fish and set aside.

Put the butter, plain flour and spring onions in another pan and heat gently until the butter has melted, stirring regularly. Continue to cook for 1 to 2 minutes then gradually whisk in the milk using a balloon whisk if you have one. Bring to the boil, stirring to avoid any lumps and sticking to the bottom of the pan. Cook for 3 to 4 minutes until thickened. Take off the heat then stir in the mixed fish, peas and cheese.

On a lightly floured surface roll out the pastry until it is the thickness of a £1 coin. Line the foils, pressing gently with your fingers to ensure the pastry has covered the foils. Cut out the pie lids at the same time, using the top of an empty foil as a template. Now fill each pie with the fish mixture until around two thirds full and top with a tablespoon of the mashed potato. Place the cut out lid on the top of each pie and crimp the pastry to seal the edges. Poke a little hole in the middle of the lids then brush the pastry with beaten egg. Place the pies in the oven for about 25 to 30 minutes, or until golden brown.

To serve

Enjoy with a green salad, crushed minted peas and a cold glass of Chablis.

Making
HEADLINES

A strong local following – in combination with home-grown staff, owners and food – lends this family-run café and bistro a truly special atmosphere.

The Press Café and Bistro got both a name and an unusual venue from the former newspaper office that it's housed in. Brothers Grant and Paul Hughes opened the venture in 2016 in their home town, Cupar, after transforming the centuries-old building into a warm and welcoming eatery. You'll find The Press tucked away down a little pend, off the main drag but at the heart of the town. On entering, the usual restaurant experience is almost reversed, since you walk through the open kitchen first to reach the dining area, via the bar. Exposed sandstone walls surround the contemporary seating which is arranged over a ground and a mezzanine floor. The open space is flooded with natural light, or cosily candlelit in winter evenings, making the transition from daytime café to afternoon and evening bistro relaxed and natural.

The Press is open for breakfasts featuring baked goodies, lunch from the bistro-style menu or a range of fresh hot filled ciabattas, and dinner on Thursday, Friday and Saturday evenings from a luxurious selection of dishes to reflect the season and the produce available. The kitchen's focus – which Paul, a professional chef for nearly twenty years who trained at Elmwood Catering College, heads up – is on locally sourced, high quality ingredients that have generally been grown or reared within a ten mile radius. Cupar is a small market town surrounded by some of Scotland's best farmland, so meat, dairy, fruit and vegetables abound from nearby suppliers and the local artisan butcher. Grant and Paul's team of ten also hail from the town and its neighbouring villages.

Some of this team are family members too; the boys' mum does all the baking and their nephew works in the kitchen part-time as well. The Hughes brothers have worked locally together for years; Grant's very first job at 15 was in a restaurant which he then ran with Paul between 2010 and 2013. Such is their reputation in Cupar that people came along to The Press when it was newly opened, having been customers at their previous restaurant. Grant and Paul will be expanding on their success very soon with another unique venture – this time in a historic local mansion house owned by the National Trust – so it's onwards and upwards, but always with their town and its people at heart.

The Press
ROAST BREAST OF BARBARY DUCK

We serve our duck breast with broccoli, carrot, kale, peas and sweet potato purée with an orangey twist. Chef's tip: to sear the duck, place it skin-side down in a cold pan and then turn the heat on.

Preparation time: 10 minutes | Cooking time: 40 minutes | Serves: 2

Ingredients

1 sweet potato

500ml orange juice

1 orange, zested

2 female duck breasts

1 head of broccoli

2 carrots

Small bunch of kale

100g frozen peas

50g butter

For the vinaigrette:

100g raspberries

100ml vinegar

3 tbsp honey

Small bunch of fresh basil

½ tsp Maldon salt

¼ tsp cracked black pepper

200ml pomace oil

Method

Peel and dice the sweet potato, then boil in the orange juice. Once soft, drain three quarters of the liquid off. Add the orange zest then purée in a blender with the remaining liquid. Season to taste then set aside and keep warm.

Place the duck breasts skin-side down in a cold pan and turn the heat on. Pan fry the duck until the skin is crispy then turn over to sear the other side. Drain off any excess fat and place in the oven skin-side down for 10 minutes at 180°c. If you don't want the duck pink, roast for a further 5 to 10 minutes.

Meanwhile, blanch the broccoli in salted water and peel the carrots into ribbons. Remove the stalks from the kale then mix the kale, peas, carrots and broccoli together.

Remove the duck from the oven and let it rest.

For the vinaigrette

Put the raspberries, vinegar, honey, basil, salt and pepper into a food processor, start blending everything together and then slowly pour the oil in and continue to blend for approximately 45 seconds or until emulsified.

Heat the butter in a pan then sauté the mixed vegetables for 2 minutes, maintaining a slight crunch for texture.

To serve

Dot the sweet potato purée in the centre and around the edge of the plate, place the vegetables in the centre on the purée, then slice the duck breast into three pieces and place on top of the vegetables.

Pride of PLAICE

On the south coast of Fife, a hotel and family home has been given a new lease of life thanks to an award-winning restaurant with local seafood at its heart.

Situated on the shore of the River Forth, underneath the stunning Hawkcraig Cliffs, Room with a View is run by partners Hannah and Tim. The restaurant is on the ground floor of a Victorian hotel dating back to 1891 that was Hannah's childhood home, and has been owned by her family since 1977. With the help of her mum, who still runs the hotel, and her partner, Hannah decided to take the plunge in 2006 to set up the restaurant, bringing new character to the beauty spot.

With Hannah running front of house and Tim as the head chef, the pair decided to showcase the best of local fish and seafood. Changing regularly, the small menu features only fish bought from H.S Murray Fishmonger in Inverkeithing, and a vegetarian option. With little meat in sight, Hannah and Tim have brought a new approach to eating out by celebrating Scottish seafood and produce. All of their ingredients are 100% local, and the menu also boasts a selection of hand-crafted desserts. Room With A View also has its own take on a tasting menu, in the form of hampers that feature a selection of either starters or desserts, offering a unique way for people to get a taste of everything the restaurant has to offer.

With only 24 seats, the small dining room is a romantic and intimate setting where guests can relax and enjoy their food, decorated in keeping with the hotel's Victorian heritage. There's also a lounge area where guests can relax and whet their appetite. The friendly and comfortable feel of the restaurant is very important to Hannah seeing as she grew up there! For sunnier days, the garden overlooking the bay is the perfect place to enjoy drinks and al fresco dining.

Being off the beaten track, Room with a View is so secluded that many people go there to escape their busy lives and experience the beauty of the Scottish countryside and taste of local seafood. In opening the restaurant, Hannah and Tim have created a new attraction for the area while preserving the welcoming and homely atmosphere that has always existed at the hotel by keeping it in the family. Room with a View is truly a home away from home.

Room with a View

LOBSTER AND SCALLOP ROE BISQUE

Lobster bisque has always been a firm favourite at Room with a View, and adding scallop roe definitely enhances the dish. We found that people were unsure of eating scallop roe, which is a shame when they are so full of flavour! We are so lucky in Scotland to have excellent lobster and scallops on our doorstep.

Preparation time: 20 minutes | Cooking time: 25 minutes | Serves: 6-8

Ingredients

For the lobster and scallop roe mix:

600-800g whole lobster, shelled and diced

500g scallop roe

1 small onion, diced

1 tsp olive oil

2 cloves of garlic, chopped

2 tsp smoked paprika

1 bay leaf

800g chopped tomatoes

250ml fish stock

250ml vegetable stock

For the roux:

100g salted butter

100g gluten-free plain flour

50ml brandy

100ml double cream

To serve:

Crusty bread

Crème fraîche

Method

For the lobster and scallop roe mix

Sauté the lobster meat, scallop roe and onion in a pan with the olive oil. Add the garlic, smoked paprika and bay leaf. Stir gently on low heat for around 3 minutes and try not to brown the ingredients. Add the chopped tomatoes, fish stock and vegetable stock and then bring to the boil. Simmer for 15 minutes. Remove from the heat and leave to cool for around 10 minutes. After cooling, blend the mixture until smooth.

For the roux

Melt the butter in a pan and then add the flour to create a smooth paste. On a gentle heat, slowly add the lobster and scallop roe mixture to the roux and keep adding until you have a smooth mixture. Strain the mixture through a fine sieve. After sieving, put the mixture back on the heat. Add the brandy and the cream and heat to 87°c, making sure not to boil. Serve in a bowl with crusty bread and a drizzle of crème fraîche.

Making
THEIR MARK

A continental market with a Scottish heart, Stockbridge Market – and those in Grassmarket and Leith that followed – bring proudly independent traders and great atmosphere together.

Stockbridge Market was launched in September 2011 by husband and wife team Beth Berry and Jean Francois Toulouze (fondly known as Jeff). Jean has been a street trader in Edinburgh for 25 years and traded at various markets, but had the ambition and experience to run a great market of his own. With Beth's background in business analysis and database design they make a perfect team.

They are of course inspired by continental markets and want to bring their customers a true market experience. The various small local independent businesses who trade with them represent a large number of countries and a diverse food offering, not to mention the various crafts on offer. Looking for a present? Choose from handmade jewellery, the work of local artists, Indian artefacts, dog couture, handmade soaps and lotions…the list goes on!

One of the market's mottos is 'eat, meet, greet or treat' and you can see why the first time you visit. There is something for everyone, and little touches like setting up tables and chairs, and very often having buskers play in the area, are provided to enhance the community feel of the market. You can find hot food from all over the world at many street traders' stalls and enjoy lunch al fresco, or buy produce to take home and cook up some fantastic meals.

Street food options include Japanese dumplings from Kaori Simpson's stall – the precursor to Harajuku Kitchen – alongside French crepes, Kenyan and Tanzanian food, Spanish paella and Greek barbecue to name just a few. The delicious produce on offer ranges from meat, fresh fish and game to artisanal French bread, fruit and vegetables, home bakes, jams and chutneys, cheeses (French, local and Italian), quality alcohols, Scotch eggs, salads, chocolates, oils, sauces and much more.

Not content to rest on their laurels, Beth, Jeff and their team have gone on to open markets in the centre of town in Grassmarket and down by the water in Leith. You can find full details on their website, or visit every weekend all year round. "It's a much more personal approach to shopping," says Beth, "and you'll never hear 'unexpected item in the bagging area' from our traders!" Each market is truly a destination for all the family and somewhere to enjoy a great day out.

THE OLIVE STALL

THREE for £10

Stockbridge Market
SMOKED FISH RISOTTO

A super easy recipe using the finest Caithness Smokehouse products, for a true taste of Scotland. The haddock is landed fresh in Scrabster and the salmon comes from the west coast of Sutherland. Try nibbling on Caithness' smoked mussels with a chilled glass of wine as an aperitif – superb.

Preparation time: 10 minutes | Cooking time: 45 minutes | Serves: 6

Ingredients

1.1 litres organic stock (chicken, fish or vegetable)

1 large onion

2 cloves of garlic

2 tbsp olive oil

1 packet of Caithness Smokehouse smoked butter

400g risotto rice

2 wine glasses of dry white vermouth (dry Martini or Noilly Prat) or dry white wine

For a smoked salmon risotto:

1 tub of Caithness Smokehouse smoked salmon pâté

1 packet of Caithness Smokehouse hot smoked salmon

For a smoked trout risotto:

1 tub of Caithness Smokehouse smoked trout pâté

1 packet of Caithness Smokehouse hot smoked trout

For a smoked haddock and pea risotto:

1 packet of Caithness Smokehouse hot smoked haddock

250g petit pois

Large handful of parsley (optional)

Method

Heat the stock while you peel and finely chop the onion and garlic. In a separate pan, heat the oil and a small knob of the smoked butter over a low heat, then add the onions and garlic and fry gently for about 15 minutes, or until softened but not coloured.

Add the rice and turn up the heat. The rice will now begin to lightly fry, so keep stirring it. After 1 minute it will look slightly translucent. Add the vermouth or wine and keep stirring – it will smell fantastic. Any harsh alcohol flavours will evaporate and leave the rice with a tasty essence.

If you are making a smoked haddock and pea risotto, lightly poach the fish in milk then strain, set the fish aside, and combine the milk with the stock.

Once the vermouth or wine has cooked into the rice, add your first ladleful of hot stock. Turn the heat down to a simmer so the rice doesn't cook too quickly on the outside. Keep adding ladles of stock, stirring and almost massaging the creamy starch out of the rice, allowing each ladleful to be absorbed before adding the next. This will take around 15 minutes. Taste the rice to check whether it's cooked. Carry on adding stock until the rice is soft but with a slight bite. Don't forget to check the seasoning carefully. If you run out of stock before the rice is cooked, add some boiling water.

Remove the pan from the heat, add another knob of smoked butter, then stir well. Now is the time to fork the tub of smoked salmon or trout pâté through the risotto, and flake the packet of smoked salmon or trout over the top. For the smoked haddock and pea risotto, add the poached fish you set aside earlier as well as the petit pois and some freshly chopped parsley if using.

Place a lid on the risotto pan and allow it to sit for 2 minutes. This is the most important part of making the perfect risotto, as this is when it becomes outrageously creamy and silky like it should be. After the 2 minutes, serve and enjoy while the risotto retains its beautiful texture.

The DIRECTORY

These great businesses have supported the making of this book; please support and enjoy them.

Akva
129 Fountainbridge
Edinburgh
EH3 9QG
Telephone: 0131 290 2500
Email: akva@bodabar.com
Swedish bar, restaurant and venue with a fantastic beer garden overlooking Union Canal. A welcoming warm space for big and small parties.

Arcade Bar, Haggis and Whisky House
48 Cockburn Street
Edinburgh
EH1 1PB
Telephone: 0131 220 1297
Website: www.arcadepub.co.uk
Historic pub transformed into a gastropub serving Scottish food and drink, focusing on haggis, whisky and a friendly welcome.

Clarinda's Tea Room
69 Canongate
Edinburgh
EH8 8BS
Telephone: 0131 557 1888
Good old-fashioned breakfasts, lunches, teas and cakes in a traditional tea room on the Royal Mile.

David Lowrie Fish Merchants Ltd
Unit 2d Netherton Industrial Estate
St Monans
KY10 2DW
Telephone: 01333 730770 / 07860 686042
Email: lowriefish@gmail.com
Website: www.lowriefish.co.uk
Family-run business championing Scottish seafood, providing the hospitality industry with the freshest and best from catch to kitchen.

Eat Me Ltd.
By Lesley-Anne Henderson
Telephone: 07940 198622
Email: info@eat-me-ltd.com
Customised cakes with classic cocktail flavourings, designed and created by Lesley in Edinburgh for any occasion in the UK that deserves such a deliciously decadent combo! Find Eatmeltd on Facebook for quotes, orders and more.

Edinburgh Larder & Larder Go
11-15 Blackfriars Street
Edinburgh
EH1 1NB
Telephone: 0131 556 6922
Website: www.edinburghlarder.co.uk
A hub for seasonal Scottish produce in the heart of Edinburgh offering a warm welcome and delicious food.

Fazenda Rodizio Bar & Grill

102 George Street
Edinburgh
EH2 3DF
Telephone: 0131 215 1234
Email: edinburgh@fazenda.co.uk
Website: www.fazenda.co.uk
Offering all the tradition behind the unique Brazilian way of serving, Fazenda is the perfect setting for a dining experience like no other.

Fhior

36 Broughton Street
Edinburgh
EH1 3SB
Telephone: 0131 477 5000
Website: www.fhior.com
Fine food and hospitality delivered with passion and skill but without pretension.

Forgan's St Andrews

110-112 Market Street
St Andrews
KY169PB
Telephone: 01334 466973
Website:
www.forgans.co.uk/st-andrews
Restaurant housed in a unique 19th century factory bringing the best of Scottish culture to St Andrews with quality food, live music events and a friendly welcome.

Gannet and Guga

Unit 2
3 East Market Street Arches
Edinburgh
EH88FS
Telephone: 0131 558 1762
Website: gannetandguga.com
Gourmet sandwich bar bringing imagination and quality ingredients together to create something special for Edinburgh's lunchtimes.

Harajuku Kitchen Japanese Bistro

10 Gillespie Place
Edinburgh
EH10 4HS
Telephone: 0131 281 0526
Website:
www.harajukukitchen.co.uk
Edinburgh's first authentic Japanese restaurant, fusing traditional family recipes with fine cooking and award-winning flair.

Joseph Pearce's

23 Elm Row
Edinburgh
EH7 4AA
Telephone: 0131 556 4140
Email: jp@bodabar.com
A neighbourhood bar that's equally welcoming for tourists and locals. Pop in for a beer, cocktail or some lovely Swedish and Scottish food.

Kilted Lobster Restaurant

112 St Stephen Street
Edinburgh
EH3 5AD
Telephone: 0131 220 6677
Website: www.kiltedlobster.com
Boutique Scottish seafood restaurant with a social conscience.

Leo's Beanery

23a Howe Street
Edinburgh
EH3 6TF
Telephone: 0131 556 8403
Website: www.leosbeanery.co.uk
Family-oriented café serving great food and great coffee, inspired by Australia and the founders' grandparents. Also does event catering under the name Leo and Ted.

The Lioness of Leith

21-25 Duke Street
Edinburgh
EH6 8HH
Telephone: 0131 629 0580
Website:
www.thelionessofleith.co.uk
Bar and bistro serving up gourmet burgers made with top quality produce, local beers, quality wines, a large range of spirits and an inventive array of cocktails in a lovingly renovated Leith pub.

Loch Leven's Larder

Channel Farm
Kinross
KY13 9HD
Telephone: 01592 841000
Website:
www.lochlevenslarder.com
Haven of fresh produce and wholesome food at the heart of a family farm.

Mussel Inn

61-65 Rose Street
Edinburgh
EH2 2NH
Telephone: 0844 683 3328
Website: www.mussel-inn.com
Award-winning Scottish seafood restaurant serving sustainably sourced, rope-grown mussels and freshly prepared dishes, to be enjoyed al fresco or in the recently refurbished interior.

The Newport Restaurant
1 High Street
Newport-on-Tay
DD6 8AB
Telephone: 01382 541449
Website:
www.thenewportrestaurant.co.uk
Friendly award-winning restaurant on the banks of the River Tay, serving modern British food in a relaxed environment.

North Port
8 North Port
Perth
PH1 5LU
Telephone: 01738 580867
Website: www.thenorthport.co.uk
Friendly restaurant showcasing carefully selected ingredients supplied by local breeders, growers and foragers to create refined and inventive dishes.

Pickering's Gin at Summerhall Distillery
Summerhall Distillery
Summerhall
Edinburgh
EH9 1PL
Telephone: 0131 290 2901
Website: www.pickeringsgin.com
Edinburgh's first exclusive gin distillery for over 150 years. Distilling, bottling, labelling and waxing a range of award-winning Pickering's Gins from the Southside arts complex, Summerhall.

The Pie Not? Bistro
135 Comiston Road
Edinburgh
EH10 6AQ
Telephone: 0131 629 1200
Website: www.pienot.co.uk
Welcoming neighbourhood bistro, serving breakfast, lunch and dinner with handmade pies as the star attraction.

The Press Café and Bistro
15-17 George Inn Pend
Crossgate
Cupar
KY15 5HA
Telephone: 01334 208384
Website:
www.thepresscafebistro.com
Warm and welcoming eatery housed in a former newspaper office, serving locally sourced and seasonally inspired café and bistro food.

Room with a View Restaurant
Forth View Hotel
Hawkcraig Point
Aberdour
Fife
KY3 0TZ
Telephone: 01383 860402
Website: www.
roomwithaviewrestaurant.co.uk
Family-run seafood restaurant in a unique location serving fresh, seasonal and local food in an intimate dining room overlooking the River Forth and Edinburgh.

At The Market Ltd
Telephone: 0131 261 6181
Email: traderstall@aol.com
Website:
www.stockbridgemarket.com
Small local farmers' markets, continental but with a Scottish heart.

Every Saturday:
Leith Market
Dock Place
Edinburgh
EH6 6LU
Grassmarket Market
Central Reservation
Edinburgh
EH1 2JR

Every Sunday:
Stockbridge Market
Saunders Street
Edinburgh
EH3 6TQ